Rebecca Huntley is a Gen-Xer. She has a PhD in Gender Studies, has worked as an academic and a political staffer, and is now a freelance writer. She is married and lives in Sydney.

The **WORLD ACCORDING** to

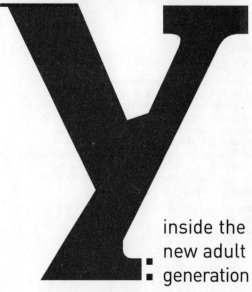

Y: inside the new adult generation

ReBeCCA HUNTLeY

ALLEN&UNWIN

First published in 2006

Copyright © Rebecca Huntley 2006

Allen & Unwin
83 Alexander Street
Crows Nest NSW 2065
Australia
Phone: (61 2) 8425 0100
Fax: (61 2) 9906 2218
Email: info@allenandunwin.com
Web: www.allenandunwin.com

National Library of Australia
Cataloguing-in-Publication entry:

Huntley, Rebecca.
   The world according to Y : inside the new adult generation.

   Includes index.
   ISBN 1 74114 845 6.

   1. Generation Y. 2. Intergenerational relations. I. Title.

305.23

Set in 11/5 pt Minion by Bookhouse, Sydney
Printed by McPherson's Printing Group, Maryborough, Victoria

10 9 8 7 6 5 4 3 2 1

Y: Contents

Acknowledgments   vii

1: From X to Y   1

2: Chicks before dicks, bros before 'hos   24

3: Germaine Greer has left the *Big Brother* house   41

4: Mr Right or Mr Right Now?   58

5: Maybe forever   74

6: A job for life   88

7: The world is a fucked-up place   103

8: It's painful to be sexy   120

9: We decide what's cool   143

10: The searching thing   159

11: The future's so bright, I gotta wear shades   177

Endnotes   189

Index   215

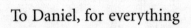

To Daniel, for everything

Acknowledgments

First and foremost I want to thank all the members of Generation Y who shared their ideas, thoughts and personal stories with me. In a world where young people get paid serious money for their opinions by market researchers, you took the time and effort to answer my questions in exchange for little more than a cup of coffee or a slice of cake. I hope this book does you justice and helps start a productive conversation between the generations about our shared future.

There are many people who provided me with information and research. I want to thank Dianna Andoni from Amnesty International Australia, Lucy Quarterman from Oxfam/Community Aid Abroad, Ani Wierenga and the Australian Youth Research Centre, Marc L'Huillier and Sweeney Research, Ruth Webber, Meredith Jones and John Wakefield.

A number of friends and colleagues read early drafts and made important contributions. I want to thank Felicity Johnston, Aaron Dibdin, Petra Stirling, Kath Albury, Ariadne Vromen, Stephanie Abbott, Hannah Cole and Jo Fox. Other friends went beyond the call of duty to help me track down young people to interview. I want to thank Moksha Watts,

Claudine Lyons, Julia Quilter, Ilona Tar, Simone Moss and all the Young Aussie Mums. Others like Natasha Cica and Catharine Lumby were always there when I needed them.

Hugh Mackay's work is a model for any researcher who wants to produce humane, thoughtful and relevant work on our society. In addition to that, his advice was invaluable. His endorsement of this book means a lot. I also want to thank Mia Freedman and Bernard Salt for their generous words endorsing this book.

On a personal note, I want to thank Emily, Graham and my mother Marisa. Your unflagging support makes a writer's life possible.

Thanks to Alex Nahlous for being such a wonderful soul and conscientious editor. And to Zoë Sadokierski for crouching in a dark toilet (don't ask . . .) to produce such an original and cool cover for the book.

I am indebted to Rebecca Kaiser for her wisdom, enthusiasm and humour. Authors get the public acclaim but little thanks ever goes to the commissioning editor who sees merit in an idea and supports that idea into book form. Thank you for making this happen and for always paying for coffee.

CHAPTER 1

From X to Y

»

The kids have got their own thing going.
Good. 'The edge' is over.
DOUGLAS COUPLAND, AUTHOR OF *GENERATION X*

Each generation is a new people.
ALEXIS DE TOCQUEVILLE

ON SEPTEMBER 11 2001, I was sitting in my living room, having just returned from the first session of a fear of flying course I was doing. The latest episode of *The West Wing* was suddenly disrupted by a news flash about a plane ploughing into the Twin Towers on a bright New York morning. My family sat glued to the TV in horror and disbelief for the next five hours. The temperature of the world seemed to change overnight and 'terrorism' became a priority issue in remote and sheltered Australia.

As disturbing as September 11 was for every person who watched it happen on TV, for older generations this wasn't the first vision of mass destruction they have witnessed that shaped their worldview in profound and lasting ways. The GI and Silent generations have their images of the Holocaust and Hiroshima. The Boomers remember napalm bombings in Vietnam. Generation X, of which I am a younger member, grew up familiar with sepia-toned mushroom clouds and the threat of nuclear extinction in fifteen minutes flat. Those Grim Reaper ads on TV caused us all to fear a sexual black plague brought on by the spread of AIDS. But for members of Generation Y—commonly defined as young men and women born in or after 1982[1]—September 11 was the most dramatic global event of their lives so far.

Generation Y reacted to September 11 in a way that says a lot about Yers, their present attitudes and future direction. Most of them have only known a peaceful world, a world of quick and effortless techno-wars that are always won by America and her allies. They have only known a prosperous world, where the Dow Jones keeps going up and people only get wealthier. They were born and raised in a global society where consumerism and capitalism are natural conditions and go largely unchallenged. To them, technology is their natural ally, a necessity rather than a luxury, the solution to all imaginable problems.[2]

September 11 was an event that threatened this new generation's sense of peace and prosperity. Monuments of corporate power were destroyed in a country whose economic and military dominance is practically unassailable. All the advanced technology in the world couldn't stop it from happening (although it ensured we got to watch it unfold live to air). The confidence of this rising generation of young men and women could have been fatally undermined by this event—but wasn't. September 11 did little to dampen the spirits of American youth, for example. A Harris Interactive Poll conducted one year after the attacks showed that American students remained optimistic about reaching future goals and did not have increased fears of a personal experience with terrorism. Many wanted to get on with their lives and not 'linger in the shadows of S 11'.[3] Drake Bennett, in his article on volunteerism, found that instead of cowing them, the attacks provoked 'a general sense of solidarity and national duty' amongst young Americans.[4]

Young Australians share the sentiments of their American contemporaries. Yes, there are parts of the world that are no-go zones due to terrorism (an annoying thought for a generation of compulsive travellers), but Generation Y's belief in its future possibilities and sense of personal freedom hasn't been curtailed in any serious way by the terrorist attacks in America, or indeed by those that occurred closer to home in Bali. Even the 2006 London bombings (in which both the perpetrators and victims were predominantly young people) seemed to have concerned but not panicked this emerging generation of young adults. Generation Y accepts, almost matter of factly, that living in today's world means you have to live with uncertainty.

In their study of wellbeing after September 11, researchers from the Australian Centre on Quality of Life found that younger people, especially young men, were less likely to say they were affected by September 11 than older people.[5] My own conversations with young people suggest a similar conclusion. Steve, a young law student recently back from trekking around South America, doesn't feel as if events like Bali and S 11 affected him 'one bit'. He says, 'It affected the way I see world politics but not the way I think or view other people.' Laura, a young journalist, shares that view. September 11 didn't undermine her sense of security or wellbeing or stop her from travelling to Europe. Kirsten Hagon, Australia's Youth Representative to the United Nations in 2001, was in New York when the planes hit the World Trade Center. Did her priorities change? 'Not really,' she stated, in a report on her UN trip. For Kirsten, September 11 was a reason for action and hope rather than inaction and fear. She believes only her generation's commitment to removing poverty and intolerance will ensure international peace and security and a world where events like S 11 don't happen again.

> *I still think young people have the passion and the optimism and the desire to make a difference. The more we are able to participate today, the sooner we can start helping to solve the problems which plague our world and work for a better tomorrow.*[6]

In Australia, Generation Y's anger around S 11 was less about the event itself than the reaction of the United States government and its allies. Many young adults have reacted negatively to the media hype around the tragedy and the relentless and insensitive use of images of death and destruction to sell papers and increase TV ratings. And whilst this was Generation Y's first exposure to international terrorism on a grand scale, most Yers were aware that in so many other places around the world this kind of stuff happens all the time. For many of them, September 11 intensified their desire to enjoy life right now.

So it seems that even the most audacious and terrifying acts of public violence can't dent the ambition and optimism of what demographers Neil Howe and William Strauss call 'the Next Great Generation'.[7]

Fast forward from September 11, 2001 to the beginning of 2003. I decided to return to casual university teaching, this time tutoring 18-year-olds in culture and communications at a regional university. Since I started teaching nearly a decade ago, I have run courses on everything from constitutional law to film studies. Every year my students seemed to get younger and younger. But suddenly in 2003, the gap between us felt like an abyss. These young people are something else. The differences relate not just to the music they listen to or the clothes they wear. The more striking differences are in terms of their basic attitudes and expectations about a whole range of issues—sex, marriage, friendship, family, politics, work, technology and the future. This is a generation with a distinctly different worldview to mine. I started to believe that these differences were worth exploring on their own terms and from the point of view of a member of Generation X.

Thinking about Generation Y has forced me to consider my own generational profile, what it means to be Generation X, that age cohort born between the early 1960s and the late 1970s. Defining X is an important step because, as Howe and Strauss found, despite a few similarities in behaviour and attitudes, Gen Y actually 'represents a sharp break from Generation X'.[8] Instead of imitating us, Yers have reacted to our mood and our failings. This is proof that social change is not a progression along letters of the alphabet but more like a pinball in a machine, reacting (sometimes unpredictably) to the hits and misses of our society and our culture.

When the term 'Generation X' was first used by Douglas Coupland as the title for his offbeat novel, I was 19 years old, a first-year university student. If I had cared enough to consider the merit of the label, I'm sure I would have resisted attempts by anyone to define my personality on the basis of having been born in 1972. I didn't see myself as anything like the bunch of slackers and malcontents the experts claimed were typical of my generation. Now, I don't mind when I am identified as part of Generation X. I feel a sense of camaraderie with others who were born in the 1970s, whose musical tastes were shaped by the 1980s and who struggle to find a place in a world still dominated by our elders.

Watching the film *Reality Bites* on cable recently, what it means to be X became abundantly clear to me. Yes, it collapses into Hollywood romance at the end but on the way the film tries hard to capture what it was like to be a young adult in the 1990s. There is the revolt against commercialism, the alienation from a dysfunctional family, the reliance on an alternative and chosen family of friends and lovers. The film's protagonists are young adults with crushing student loans and university degrees who find themselves in minimum-wage jobs at The Gap and McDonalds. There is a resistance to marriage, feelings of shock and horror that people from high school are having babies already. These protagonists are finding their way through the post-university malaise without any guidance from heroes or role models, or any help from their Baby Boomer parents who tell them times are tough, swallow your pride and take that job at $5 an hour.

The feeling of hopelessness is there too. In her Valedictorian speech, Lelaina, played by Winona Ryder, asks her audience of parents and peers: 'How are we going to repair all the damage we've inherited? The answer is . . . I don't know.' The grand, youthful ambitions of the Boomers no longer seem relevant or realistic. These characters are dubious about 'making the world a better place'. They know that whatever they choose to do with their life, however meaningful to them, isn't going to 'end world hunger or save the planet'. Ten years on and the characters in *Reality Bites* would still be grappling with career and commitment issues, trying to balance the needs of economic stability with personal fulfilment. They would probably be renters rather than mortgagees, in de facto relationships rather than married with kids, some still reliant on parents to get by financially, most still reliant on friends to get by at all. They may well be working in a job totally unrelated to their university degree.

There is no doubt in Howe and Strauss's statement that X has 'the worst reputation of all living generations'.[9] It has been called the 'Me Generation', too selfish and self-absorbed to commit to a marriage, children, saving money or a permanent job. We postpone taking on the responsibilities of adulthood to the last possible moment, making us 'adultescents'.[10] More sympathetic commentators have described us as the 'Options Generation'. We keep our options open in all aspects of our lives, 'choosing' to postpone long-term commitments in favour of short-term goals and stop-gap measures.[11] Generation X has also been characterised as deeply pessimistic, an entire generation who saw the world through grey-coloured glasses. We grew up fearing nuclear annihilation, unemployment and AIDS, with little confidence in the future of the world or our own. Politicians weren't providing the answers and neither were our parents. There were no grand causes to believe in (expect perhaps salvaging the environment). We were highly cynical about anything and everything.

Our expectations in life were lower than our parents'— and for good reason too. X was the first generation to begin to feel the force of what journalist Simon Castles calls 'the negative consequences of two decades of extraordinary economic and social change'.[12] Even now we wield much less economic power than the generations ahead of us. We are mostly locked out of the housing market and haven't experienced the kind of job security that was common in countries like Australia when our parents first exited school and university. In fact, a university degree, something that practically guaranteed success for our parents, would no longer ensure graduate Xers financial prosperity or career advancement. Strauss and Howe call us 'The Thirteenth Generation', a reflection of how unlucky we have been to be born and raised during such a dismal time in our recent history.[13] Faced with such difficulties, life has become all about survival. In order to make it in an unforgiving world, we have had to become comfortable with change and adopt a flexible and pragmatic approach to everything. We get by on talent, luck and the benevolence of others (usually our parents).

Considering Generation Y from the point of view of a Gen-Xer, it is easy to be suspicious, judgmental and even a bit jealous. We felt abandoned whereas they have felt treasured and protected. Howe and Strauss believe that Gen X 'had reason to feel like a throwaway generation whose problems older people ignored', whereas Gen Y 'have always felt themselves to be the focus of public attention'.[14] We have a deep-rooted sceptical outlook[15] whereas Generation Y thinks anything and everything is possible. They are far more confident about their own lives and the world's long-term survival. Social commentator Hugh Mackay summarises the mood contrast between X and Y by comparing the attitudes of a 19-year-old in 1980 and 2000.[16] According to Mackay, in 1980 the average 19-year-old feared nuclear annihilation and saw life as grim and uncertain. His concerns about the future of the planet were tied up with anxieties about his own future, particularly his career prospects. Time-travel two decades forward and the average 19-year-old is confident, both about her future and the future more generally. She puts a big premium in having fun. She is more relaxed and capable of taking uncertainty in her stride without complaint. So in one generation we have seen a basic attitude shift from pessimism to optimism. This is intriguing if we consider that many of the problems facing our society in 1980—environmental degradation, violence and war, family breakdowns, employment insecurity, third-world poverty and so on—still exist in this millennium. It seems that Generation Y is more capable than X at facing these problems—or more effective at ignoring them.

There is an irresistible urge when defining a generation of young people to make comparisons (often uncomplimentary) with older generations ('young people these days,

I don't know...' etc).[17] I have tried my best to avoid the tendency amongst those over the age of 35 to see young people as 'a problem that needs fixing'[18]—girls with eating disorders, boys without role models, homeless and drug-addicted teenagers, 20-somethings who are underemployed and oversexed, the list goes on. As Eckersley observes, older generations often see the world 'in a state of moral decline' and tend to blame the young for this decline.[19] I do compare and contrast Y with the X and Baby Boomer generations throughout this book. In fact, part of this book's central theme hinges on how Y differs from X and how it is shaped by the parent generation. But whilst these influences, tensions and differences are important and interesting, Yers certainly deserve to be considered on their own terms.

What is Generation Y? The term is clumsy, and suggests that it picks up where X left off, which is not the case. It has been given many names—the Net Generation, the Millennials, the Dotcoms and the Thumb Generation (referring to their dexterity with remote controls, computer keyboards and mobile phones), and Echo-Boomers (as the product, both biologically and socially, of their Baby Boomer parents). Yers have been described as the Paradoxical Generation, due to their seemingly contradictory approach to life (they drink and take drugs but eat organic food, they are obsessed with technology but fear it is depriving them of deeper personal relationships, they want to get married but resist settling down with a partner).[20] I have struggled to come up with my own term for this new group. I once dreamt about a possible name for them—Generation Blue Sky. It reflects the optimism and ambition of these young adults, the sense that their horizons are big and the possibilities endless. But like all the labels it seems to fall short of capturing what this generation is all about. So I have stuck with the term Generation Y.

Whatever you call them, there are certainly lots of them. They are the largest youth generation in history. In the United States, they encompass more than 70 million people and are almost three times the size of Generation X.[21] In Australia, Generation Y isn't super-sized like in the United States. There are 1 119 755 people in the 18–25 age bracket compared with 2 025 351 in the much larger Gen X 26–39 age bracket.[22] However, this million-plus will form the bulk of the adult population within the next 20 years and may steamroll Gen-Xers in the process, running over them in both public and private institutions. Generation Y's sheer size will make sure it makes its mark on the world in a way Generation X never did. We will have to understand their mindset in order to navigate our own future.

In order to understand why they are who they are, we need to understand their past, the world they were born into and grew up in. As children, their family environment was one of curious contradiction. Yers are mostly planned children rather than 'Saturday night specials', born to older parents who wanted to conceive (and sometimes had difficulties). They were usually born into small families, growing up alone or with only one sibling.[23] All this has made them feel special and wanted. The decade of their childhood, the 1980s, was also a time when public fears about child abuse and abduction emerged with some force. The 'Stranger Danger' message was extended to include 'Everyone Danger', due to rising public awareness of child abuse in previously safe havens such as churches, schools and camps. Children were clearly not safe outside home but even inside home there were threats behind every door. New child-safety devices swamped the market in the late 1980s. There were ad campaigns about unfenced swimming pools and boiling pots tumbling off stoves. This was happening at a time of increased public concern about violence in schools, youth gangs and suicides, drug abuse, teen sex and pregnancy. Whilst these were all Generation X problems, they meant that parents of young children in the 1980s became hyper-aware of all the possible threats the world might pose to their special child.

Changes in politics and culture during the 1980s mirrored this new interest in children's welfare and protection. It was an era where family values and 'the best interests of the child' became public rather than private goals. Howe and Strauss call this 'kinderpolitics', the political trend to translate concerns about children's current and future status into aggressive public policy on everything from crime to media content to welfare payments.[24] 'Kinderpolitics' was something that infused the rhetoric and policies of parties across the political spectrum and was almost impossible to rebut. Popular culture also registered this spotlight shift from adults to children. Whereas the late 1960s horror flick *Rosemary's Baby* kick-started a decade-long stint of bad-child films, the early 1980s saw kids become cute again.[25] Movies like *Baby Boom* and *Three Men and a Baby* showed how children could transform the selfish lives of adults for the better. Movies like *Home Alone* showed them as super-smart heroes without capes. And so the cultural, social and political terrain of the 1980s ensured that Generation Y became, according to Howe and Strauss, the 'healthiest and most cared-for child generation' in history.[26] And on the whole these Yers felt 'wanted, protected and worthy' of all the attention.[27]

Despite all this familial care and concern, Generation Y (like their older sisters and brothers in Generation X) experienced divorce on a widespread scale. They grew up in families of increasing complexity, with step-siblings, half-siblings, parents who remarried or re-partnered without marrying. One out of four young Australians grew up in a single-parent household. Three out of four were raised by working mothers. With two overworked parents rather than one, Yers have witnessed dissatisfaction and conflict over work and family issues. They have seen stressed mothers faced with a double shift of paid work in the marketplace and unpaid work in the home. They have seen workaholic and sometimes distant fathers who probably resisted attempts by their spouses to get them to share the domestic burden.

In many ways, the most important change to have affected this generation has been economic. Since the mid-1970s, while the costs of setting out in life (housing, education and training fees) have raced ahead of inflation, the rewards (salaries and fringe benefits for young workers) have steadily fallen behind.[28] According to youth researcher Ani Wierenga, these changes in the economy and labour market mean that young people are increasingly denied access to the markers of adulthood—work, marriage, children and buying a home.[29] This means that while the members of Generation Y enjoyed relatively comfortable childhoods, their transition to adulthood (as previous generations understand it) will be slow and difficult. Homeownership, steady salaries and permanent relationships will be the stuff of their mid to late 30s rather than their 20s. And so their young adult lives will be fun and flexible, but insecurity will always be present. Their reliance on their parents will stretch well beyond the end of school and university. On a broader economic scale, the 1980s saw the triumph not just of capitalism but also of economic rationalism (market fundamentalism, neo-liberalism, whatever name you give it). The logic of the market, the drive to consume, to earn and to spend more has infused not just the economy but also our society and our culture. Whilst many in Generation Y question, resist and reject elements of this culture of capitalism, they are all caught up in it and it shapes their attitudes and outlooks in complex and profound ways.

Generation Y's past life and current status means that it is emerging as an age cohort with some distinct, albeit still evolving, personality traits. Generation Y's first and in many ways defining attribute is its optimism. Yers seem to embody the early optimism and idealism of their Boomer parents. They are described in study after study as optimistic, idealistic, empowered, ambitious, confident, committed and passionate. They are assured about their own futures and, in many cases, the future of the world. The 2004 Spin Sweeney report found that young consumers in the 16–28 age bracket are startlingly optimistic, with three-quarters of the respondents thinking the future will be better than the past.[30] As mentioned before, Y optimism stands in stark contrast to the pessimism of Generation X. The reason for this difference relates entirely to expectations and disappointment. Members of Generation X remember the promise of a secure life, even if we were young when that promise was broken. Gen-Xers felt betrayed as a result and so we were disillusioned and cynical. As Coupland explains, 'We were all promised heaven in our lifetimes, and what we ended up with can't help but suffer in comparison.'[31] But Yers were never promised security and so they deal with insecurity with far less self-pity and anger than Xers did.

Generation Y's optimism and confidence is even more astounding when we consider the uncertain and insecure world in which Yers live. Whilst their childhoods were sheltered worlds in which their desires were eagerly met by parents and grandparents, they have emerged into an adult world where only one rule exists—the certainty of uncertainty. Hugh Mackay says this is a generation 'born into the age of uncertainty'.[32] Life events that were in the past viewed as devastating were no longer unexpected or unusual—parents getting a divorce or losing their jobs, a brother or sister committing suicide, a friend coming out as gay. Yers have grown up knowing they can't rely on so many things that were taken for granted by other generations—a job, marriage, the opportunity to have children (and to spend time with them), a family, the chance to buy your own home, an education that leads to a career, a social safety net and a secure retirement. Indeed, as a consequence of economic and social changes in the 1980s and 1990s, Generation Y is the first generation to fully experience divorce, downsizing and user-pays higher education.[33]

Insecurity and uncertainty are now part of life for all age groups. But Generation Y, with its unfailing optimism, has incorporated 'uncertainty' and 'insecurity' into its worldview and has refashioned these negatives into 'freedom' as a positive.[34] Freedom and uncertainty are the yin and yang of the Y world. Choice, options, flexibility are the buzzwords for this generation, something marketers and the manufacturers of mobile phones have long understood. When Gen-Yers want structure—in terms of work, finances, living arrangements or relationships—they do so on the condition that their independence and freedom to experiment are not curtailed.[35] They value difference, diversity and change in all aspects of their lives. George Barna states that two of the rules this generation lives by are: 'aggressively pursue diversity among people' and 'change is good'.[36] They favour mobility and movement. They are highly mobile in a physical sense, a generation of globetrotters who don't just travel for holidays and adventure but want to live and study overseas. They are highly mobile in terms of their careers, moving from company to company, from city to city, from country to country, training and retraining, shifting from one professional direction to another with a speed that frazzles their parents and older work colleagues.

In this sense, the mobile phone is an icon for this generation. In the Y world, a mobile phone is not merely a phone. It is, as described by demographer Bernard Salt, 'a personal accessory, a personal communications device, and a personal entertainment centre'.[37] It's a device for work and play, flirtation and sex, friendship and family. For Yers, their phone symbolises freedom and flexibility. More than that, your mobile phone symbolises *you*. Its make, model, colour, faceplate and ring tone (all changeable and constantly changing as fashion accessories and status symbols) reflect your personality. Daniel, a 19-year-old journalism student, believes 'Your phone says a lot about you. You contain your personality in your phone.' Your mobile is what connects you to everything so it becomes an extension of your own body. Jackie, an ambitious 23-year-old in PR, describes her mobile as 'like my right arm'.

The interaction between technology and Generation Y has been the subject of much research and public commentary. It is clearly the most technologically savvy generation yet, a group that has never known a world without remote controls, CDs, cable TV and computers.[38] Of course this has ramifications for the workplace and the marketplace. The future of communications companies and electronic manufacturers is certainly secure. But Gen Y's understanding and early adoption of new technologies goes beyond its seemingly unique capacity to program the household DVD. Generation Y's mastery of and reliance on technology has altered the way it views time and space.

Generation Y has a different perception of space because, according to Howe and Strauss, it is 'the world's first generation to grow up thinking of itself as global'.[39] The Internet and satellite television networks are just two of myriad new technologies that have made this possible. This shift hasn't just been cultural, with Gen-Yers sharing a global youth culture of music, fashion, celebrities and movies. It has been political, with the priorities of Generation Y bypassing the issues of national politics and shifting further towards a new politics that links international political problems with local community concerns. It has been personal, with Yers eager to experience life and work in other countries. The distances between issues, places, the national and the international, the personal and the global have contracted. Linked to this, and thanks to the speed in which we can now communicate with each other via these new technologies, time has also changed. Generation Y expects things to happen quickly, at the speed of MP3 downloads and text messages. The contraction of time means there is little personal space for quiet reflection and thoughtful consideration. All this combines with changing labour markets, life patterns and so forth to make planning beyond a few years' time seem a fruitless endeavour. Gen-Yers can't even commit to Stalinistic five-year plans, with many only looking ahead to the next twelve months.

There is a darker side to all this optimism, confidence and mobility. Insecurity doesn't always foster self-reliance, enterprise and creativity. Paradoxically, whilst this is a generation that values freedom, flexibility and choice, it is also far more conformist than its X predecessors. The desire to fit in, to be part of the group, which has always been present in youth culture, is especially important for Generation Y. Youth market researcher Chris Watt explains that by far the most pressing issue confronting Gen-Yers in daily life is 'the never-ending desire to be accepted, to belong'.[40] The contrast between X and Y is illustrative here.[41] There was rebellious-ness that was at the heart of X culture, a product of our pessimism and disappointment. That rebelliousness has now been eroded to the point of disappearance. Films aimed at the Y market emphasise consensus and belonging, to such a point that the culture of the insiders now dominates. Alissa

Quart makes this point in her book *Branded* which discusses teen films in the 1980s and 1990s. The heroes of 1980s teen films were the outsiders, 'the kids who rejected the established order'.[42] Take a classic Gen X film like *Pretty in Pink*. The heroine Andy, played by Molly Ringwald, is an academically gifted girl from the wrong side of the tracks who can fashion an outfit for the prom from hand-me-down dresses and thrift-shop finds. The villains? The rich and nasty popular kids with their cool cars, big houses and designer labels. Flash forward to the new millennium and the villains have now transformed into heroes in movies like *Legally Blonde* and *Bring It On*. As Quart argues, the lifestyles and ethos of the insiders, conspicuous consumption and brand placement are central to the story-lines and characters of today's teen flicks in a way that champions fitting in and getting along over independence and challenging society's rules.

Some members of Generation Y see this conformism and are disturbed by it. Meg, a 20-year-old arts graduate, feels that her generation is 'very conformist' and 'follow each other like sheep'. She says, 'We all dress the same and act the same.' Tony, an astute trainee accountant, thinks that the conformism of his generation is a product of a privileged childhood. 'We all sort of float along on our parents' money,' he says. 'Everything is handed to us on a plate.' This desire to conform, to be part of the crowd, is just one of the consequences of a childhood existence spent in a period of unprecedented prosperity and a cocoon of creature comforts. This conformism, this unquestioning, sometimes cheerful acceptance of the logic of consumerism and capitalism, is the darker side of Generation Y's optimism and confidence.

It is Generation Y's fatal flaw and may yet prove to overwhelm its more positive attributes.

Despite being only a decade or so apart in terms of age, Yers aren't like Xers, even if they are occasionally lumped in with them. There is no doubt that Yers have learned some prophetic lessons from their Xer cousins (for example, about waiting too long to get married and have children). But the world according to Y has been shaped more by the parent generation—the Baby Boomers—than it has by the previous one. It is the Boomers that have created both the conditions for Y's future success and the barriers to its full development as 'the Next Great Generation'. Boomers have nurtured, educated, funded and encouraged their Y kids—and will continue to do so. But these parents have also helped create a world where Yers will struggle to attain the kind of financial, social and employment security and independence that Boomers took for granted when they were in their 20s. Yet another paradoxical turn in the evolution of Generation Y is that despite the fact Yers are heavily influenced and continually reliant on their parents, they don't want to follow their parents' example. The Boomers' obsession with work has made Yers question whether their career is the be all and end all. Despite the Yers' consumerist urges (a direct hand-me-down from Boomer materialism), they question whether consumerism provides the answers. Yers know they don't want many of the hallmarks of their parents' existence—divorce and marital unhappiness, workaholism, stress-related illness, a life without fun, friends and meaningful relationships. They want marriages that last, quality of life and children (but not too many or too soon). They want to maintain a safety net of friends around them, even after they establish themselves in families and jobs. So whilst many commentators call them the 'Echo-Boomers', they could also equally be described as the 'Anti-Boomers'. They are feeling their way towards a life philosophy that is both shaped by and defined in opposition to the Boomers' experience.

In writing this book, I have used academic and market research, media resources as well as my own extensive interviews with more than 50 young men and women from around Australia. I tried to be broadly representative by seeking out interviewees who are gay and straight, from different social, ethnic and religious backgrounds, some married, some with children, from different parts of Australia both urban and regional. I relied on the thoughts, confessions and insights of these 50-plus Yers to bring to life the conclusions I make about this generation, the world they live in and the one they will create. Some of these young Australians have asked to remain anonymous and so I do use pseudonyms along with the real first names of my interviewees.

Of course, there will be countless young people who won't recognise themselves in the various portraits of Generation Y this book presents. There are resisters out there, who question the conformism of their peers, who reject, sometimes aggressively, the cult of consumerism, who are deeply worried about their own future and the future of the world. There are young people (especially those on low incomes and living in remote areas) who aren't connected to the Internet or who don't own a mobile phone. There are those who haven't the skills, opportunities, capital or family support to reinterpret insecurity as freedom, to travel the world for work or play. These are the members of Generation Y who may well succumb to mental illness, who will fall into an underclass that governments seem unwilling or incapable of dealing with. But diagnosing a generation necessitates generalisation. As I said at the beginning of this chapter, I never empathised with the Generation X image when it first emerged, but I relate to it now as an adult, looking back on my formative years with a more objective eye. According to youth researchers Melissa Butcher and Mandy Thomas, being part of a generation means you share 'particular memories of the contemporary moment'.[43] Whilst those memories will inevitably be shaped by other factors (gender, sexuality, race, religion, class, geography, whatever), the broader environment in which you live will make a big impression on you and your peers—whether you understand it at the time or not. So I have sought to define the general environment and attitudes of Generation Y, something that even resisters must confront in their efforts to swim against the tide.

Demographers Howe and Strauss anticipate that Generation Y will break out and attract maximum social attention around 2010.[44] But Yers have long been the subject of countless studies and surveys by market researchers who flog their findings to companies and corporations eager for the Y dollar. Over the last few years the news media has become increasingly interested in understanding this generation as its members start to leave high schools and universities, enter the workforce and the marketplace, and start to commit to long-term relationships and even parenthood. Others have 'boomeranged', moving back home to live with parents in order to save for international travel or a car. So parents, older siblings, employers, sociologists, politicians and the like are joining market researchers and their clients in asking questions about Generation Y and how it will shape our society and our future. The contradictory impulses in this generation are starting to play themselves out as Yers move gradually into adulthood, entering and interacting with public and private institutions. This book makes an early call on what this generation is like and what it will become. Of course it is still emerging and evolving. The ongoing war on terror might change them, as might a global economic downturn or sustained environmental disaster. What I do know is that it is a longer distance from X to Y than I ever thought.

CHAPTER 2

Chicks before dicks, bros before 'hos

»

DOUGLAS COUPLAND's *Generation X* tells the story of three friends Dag, Claire and Andy who have dropped off the radar to live in adjacent bungalows in Palm Springs. Through all the craziness and instability in their lives, their commitment to each other as friends is unquestioned, unshakeable, the spine of the story. The restlessness and discontent of the main character, Andy, is only soothed by the presence of his friends in his life. 'I feel calm because my friends are nearby … these creatures here in this room with me—these are the creatures I love and who love me.'[1] Andy is terminally single and his relationship with his family (who live in another state) is often difficult. Claire and Dag are the main players in his life.

Like most members of Generation X, my friends are an essential part of my world. As a child of divorced parents, I know all about the problems involved in long-term relationships. My immediate family consists of only a few people. My friends are my insurance policy against the possibility of love and family diminished or lost. They are my extended clan, a support network maintained over coffee, cocktails and brunch, connected by phone, email and text. Gen X journalist Ethan Watters argues as much in his book *Urban Tribes*, his personal investigation into why he and so many of his peers were single and childless well into their 30s. Watters found that for Generation X it was friends and acquaintances rather than spouses and family that were meeting essential needs and desires.[2] Rather than getting married straight after school or university and moving out to the suburbs like our parents did, we are drawn to cities and towns, where our friendship networks become like family arrangements.[3] We are fiercely loyal to each other, supportive, loving and in constant contact.

Even more than X, members of Generation Y are intensely tribal creatures. Young people's reliance on friendship groups is nothing new. What is new is that Generation Y expects to be committed to friends well beyond young adulthood. Hugh Mackay states that 'young adults are totally anchored to the group, and expect to be for the long haul'. He explains that:

> ... *even their sexual relationships are no threat to the solidarity of the tribe. Come what may, they expect their friends to stick by them. A failed romance? The group is balm for the soul. No work? Your friends will be there to love and support you. Your family is driving you bats? You'll always have your friends.*[4]

For Yers, friends are like family only better. They provide an escape from parental dramas and expectations. They are the first people you call if you are in trouble. Kerry is a 20-year-old Torres Strait Islander, who spent her childhood moving around Australia. Her parents are separated and living in a different city and so her friends are her substitute family. Jenny is close to her parents but they are successful, busy people so she turns to her friends for emotional support.

Pop culture has reflected this shift away from family towards friendships. When I was a teenager in the 1980s, the most successful TV sitcoms—like *The Cosby Show*, *Family Ties*, *Growing Pains* and *Who's The Boss*—centred on families. Today's popular family-based sitcoms—like *Everybody Loves Raymond* and *The Simpsons*—derive most of their humour from the idea that your family is a constant irritation and embarrassment, basically 'dysfunctional' (to use that overused term). In comparison, the 1990s onwards saw the dominance of friend-based sitcoms and dramas aimed at young viewers like *Friends*, *Sex and the City*, *Secret Life of Us*, *Seinfeld* and *Buffy the Vampire Slayer*. In these shows the key characters move in and out of relationships and their biological relations are either absent or relegated to the sidelines.

The hugely popular sitcom *Friends* enjoyed its success and longevity for a reason. It tapped into the reality that for Generation Y, as well as for X, friends are the family you get to choose. Xers were well into university when *Friends* came to Australian TV but Generation Y started watching it as teenagers. When the series began in 1994, all the characters were single, carefree and in their 20s. By the show's end, they were in their 30s, some married or in relationships, some with kids, but they had all achieved those goals in unconventional ways. The show's main romantic interests, Ross and Rachel, dated and broke up, got married and divorced, had a child together and then finally became a family in the closing minutes of the final episode. But through all the tumult and change they remained friends and their group stayed intact. Similarly, the theme of the equally successful show *Buffy the Vampire Slayer* is about the protection and the power that the friendship group provides. Buffy may be the only slayer on earth but any fan of the show will tell you she would have been dead by Series 2 if it wasn't for her pals in The Scooby Gang, there to back her up no matter what. In that show, the friendship circle has an intense and magical power that can actually save the world—over and over. TV has registered that for X and Y *the group* has eclipsed *the pair* as the dominant social unit.[5]

It's no surprise that Yers prefer to hang with their friends rather than their mums and dads. But it also seems that this generation prioritises friendships ahead of sexual relationships. In fact, a 2004 survey of young consumers in the 16–28 age bracket found that the majority of respondents put relationships with friends before relationships with their partner.[6] There is a passage at the end of Nick Hornby's *About a Boy* that reflects both a Generation Y scepticism about the durability of sexual relationships and an optimism about friendship networks. Marcus, an odd but insightful 12-year-old boy, outlines his view of personal relationships in response to a question about marriage:

> *You know when they do those human pyramids? That's the sort of model for living I'm looking at now ... You're safer as a kid if everyone's friends. When people pair off ... I don't know. It's more insecure ... I just don't think couples are the future.*[7]

Today Marcus would be 18 years old and his views would have remained the same. Friendship networks are stronger and safer than simply becoming part of a couple. For Yers, when sexual relationships happen it is often within the context of a larger friendship group. Time spent with a boyfriend or girlfriend can feel like a distraction from the really important task of socialising with your mates.[8]

If Generation Y were to have any kind of hard and fast rule, it would be 'chicks before dicks' and 'bros before 'hos'. Friends come first because unlike your family and your current relationship, they are the ones you can count on in the long run. This idea is reflected everywhere in Y culture.

Take the site www.suburbanunderground.org, which features 'A Young Person's Code of Ethics'. The central tenant of this Code illustrates the significance of friendships over sexual relationships for Generation Y. According to the Code, 'Friendship (with the implied corollaries of stability, acceptance, and an emotional and intellectual bond) takes precedence over romantic relationships (with the implied corollary of sexual relations).' Because friendship with a person wins out over a romantic relationship with that same person, romantic relationships with friends are unacceptable. What about romantic relationships with strangers? Not possible either. Romantic relationships require 'emotional vulnerability and intimacy' and 'offering this to strangers is always a big mistake'. So romantic relationships with strangers and other non-friends are unacceptable. The message is clear—friendship trumps romance every time.

For those members of Generation Y who are pessimistic about their romantic futures, close friendships are a welcome substitute for partnering up. For example, Brendan, a 22-year-old bank worker, feels that 'As someone who doesn't necessarily see himself in a relationship ever, friends are absolutely necessary.' For newly single Y women like Sarah, friends become particularly important as a major source of support after a break-up. After ending a 12-month relationship, Sarah feels that her friends are 'essential' to her life. She says 'With friends, you know they are always going to be around whereas anything could happen with a boyfriend. You have always got your friends to fall back on.'

But even for those who are happily married or in long-term relationships, a reliance on friendships remains. Lawrence is 23 years old and has been in a long-term relationship with a young woman he met on exchange. Despite the fact he and his partner live together in his parents' house, his friends provide 'a release' from work, family and also from the pressures of a serious relationship. David, who has been married for two years, feels his broad network of mates provides 'a vent' that supports rather than undermines his relationship with his wife. 'My wife isn't much of a party-goer but I am so it's good for us to have that time away from each other,' he says. For Lee-Ann, who doesn't share common interests with her de facto, friends provide her with essential social time and companionship. She says 'My friends are willing to go out if I need to whereas my partner isn't.' Other Yers feel like they can be themselves with their friends more than with their partner. Martin's partner doesn't have to 'meet the high expectations' he has of his really close friends, from whom he expects unconditional support and love, total understanding and absolute loyalty.

So while Y men and women treat romantic notions of everlasting love for a sexual partner with a heavy dose of cynicism, the idea of friendship for life is seen as absolutely possible, in fact necessary. Sexual partners come and go but friends will be with you forever. They will help you get over heartache and provide unconditional love and support. Even when Yers find a mate, friendships are maintained and still seen as essential, even to the health of their sexual relationship. In this world of uncertainty, divorce and unhappy marriages as the norm rather than the exception, notions of eternal romance and sexual love have been fatally compromised. But they haven't disappeared. Instead they have been transferred into the realm of friendships. Valuing friendships has been one of the numerous lessons learned from the example of the Boomers. Many Yers have parents who let their friendships slip away and die because they were too caught up in work and family. These parents were left isolated and lonely when their marriages collapsed. Yers' investment in friendship acts as a crucial counterweight to family and work. Their commitment to friendship is a commitment to a balanced and diverse life.

Whilst friendships are given priority broadly across Generation Y, the quality of male and female friendships remains different. The intensity of female relationships is initiated early, mostly in high school where the power of the clique overrides parental influence and rivals romantic relationships with boys. The deep bond between girls has been analysed with precision in Rosalind Wiseman's bestseller *Queen Bees and Wannabes*. In this intelligent self-help book for parents, Wiseman shows how vital female relationships are to the self-esteem and personal growth of teenage girls. These friendships are so powerful that, by contrast, early relationships with boys can't compete. Wiseman observes that 'It's hard for the awkward first crush to measure up to the ease and intimacy of girl-girl friendships.'[9]

For many Y women, even mature sexual relationships can't quite match the unqualified intimacy of friendships that stretch from childhood into adolescence and adulthood. This is a *Sex and the City* generation and young women value their female friends above all others. For example, Jenny, an outgoing and artsy 23-year-old, has a wide friendship circle formed through music and drama classes as well as work and school. She counts men in her friendship circle but it is her friendships with women that have been 'particularly strong'. Girlfriends are the ultimate confidantes; everything is disclosed about love, guys, work, play, family and of course sex. Renee, who recently got married, shares 'intimate stuff' with her best girlfriend 'that you wouldn't tell a guy'. Y women talk candidly to their girlfriends about their sex lives in a way they never would with their own sexual partner, further evidence of the special trust bestowed on friends over lovers.

This ultimate trust and intimacy between young women supports a double standard. A typical Y girl has higher moral expectations of her female friends than she does of the man in her life. In her view, men don't have a clue but her girlfriends should always know better. This faith in female friends over a male partner is reflected in Nikki Gemmell's novel *The Bride Stripped Bare*, a bestseller amongst X and Y women readers. When the leading character's husband has an affair with her best friend, she stays with the husband Cole but shuts the best friend Theo out of her life. In the final analysis it is the best friend she holds to a higher standard of conduct, rather than her life partner.

> *Theo's betrayal is magnificent, astounding, incomprehensible. It's her actions you can't understand, not Cole's. You always assumed she was the one person you'd have your whole life, not, perhaps, your mother or your husband. She's a woman, she knows the rules. Men do not.*[10]

32 Rosalind Wiseman argues that because girls are conditioned to believe that boys are born cheaters, they don't hold them to the same standard as they do their female friends. Wiseman writes 'Since girls' friendships are still often more intimate than the sexual relationships they are having with a boy, the feeling of betrayal often runs correspondingly deeper. Girls excuse boys' behaviour. They don't excuse girls' behaviour.'[11] This girl loyalty runs the other way too. For example, Meisha, a vivacious medical student, subscribes to the view that while you might cheat on your boyfriend, 'you'd never do the dirty on your friend'.

The friendships between Y men are different. Australian culture has celebrated friendships between men to the point of creating a cult of mateship. But whilst men might support each other on the football field and carry each other home after a night at the pub, their intimacy doesn't always extend to detailed conversations about life, love or sex. Author and men's movement advocate, Steve Biddulph argues that boys' friendship networks are 'awkward and oblique, lacking in intimacy and often short term'.[12] For the average Y bloke, friends provide relaxed company and jokey, laid-back banter. Biddulph says 'A subtle and elaborate code governs the humour and the put-downs' via which a young man communicates with his mates.[13]

For someone like James, a 23-year-old working in insurance, friends don't provide the intense emotional support that is so central to relationships amongst women. They provide him with 'a bit of a laugh and something to do' rather than 'an emotional thing'. Young men tend to disclose less personal information to their friends than young women do. There isn't a vocabulary for them to talk seriously and specifically about sex and relationships in a way that doesn't make everyone feel uncomfortable. If it's emotional support or advice a Y guy is after, he is more likely to confide in his girlfriend, a female friend or relative—or not at all. This pattern of disclosure to girls and non-disclosure to boys starts early. In her work with teenagers, Rosalind Wiseman found that:

> *Many boys would much rather talk to a female friend about their problems—because they fear their male friends will laugh at them or blow them off [because] asking for help is often the same as admitting you're weak and sensitive, which translates for boys into being feminine and gay.*[14]

Despite all of this, some of the Y guys I interviewed questioned my assumption that their friendships with men are less intimate than friendships between women. Aspiring journalist Daniel, 21, challenges the cliché that men don't confide in each other the way women do:

> *The idea that men don't talk to each other has always bothered me. We do but we just tend to be a lot more laid-back about it. If we've got a problem in a relationship, we'd talk about it frankly and we keep that information confidential. When we do say something, it means a lot more.*

Maybe Daniel is right. The nature of male friendship is slowly changing, altered by the growing importance of friends across Generation Y and the standard set by the intense intimacy between their female peers.

What qualities do Y men and women look for in their friendships? As with everything sought after and valued by this generation, friendships provide more flexibility and freedom than other relationships. Yers are free to 'be themselves' with their friends in a way they can't be with family or a partner. For history post-grad Liam, 24, his friends give him 'a chance to be myself, a chance to build an identity outside of family and a relationship'. Friends can give unconditional support, acceptance and advice in a way that is difficult for others who are closer or more invested. For Daney, friends provide understanding 'without moral judgments' whereas a partner or family will have their own opinion about what you should do. He says 'Friends will only do that if you ask them to.'

Diversity is another sought-after quality in Y friendships. In fact, George Barna believes that Gen-Yers 'aggressively pursue diversity among people'.[15] Their friendship groups include people they met at primary school and high school, through study and work, through other friends and ex-partners. More often than not Yers try hard to retain friendships made at a particular time and place in life long after they have moved on to something new. Many of them see that having a diverse group of friends (gay and straight, male and female, black and white) keeps life interesting. In their study of ethnic youth in western Sydney, sociologists Melissa Butcher and Mandy Thomas found that the major difference between the social experiences of immigrant parents and their Generation Y offspring 'was in the diversity of their friendship networks'.[16] Many of these young adults thought that having friends from different backgrounds was more 'open-minded' and 'more tolerant'. These kinds of friends are an exciting complement or alternative to the predictability of a relationship or the familiarity of family. (Diversity amongst this most racially and ethnically diverse generation is so well-accepted that any public lecturing or political posturing about difference and multiculturalism seems irrelevant and outdated.)

How is this essential support network maintained in the midst of a busy lifestyle? The answer is technology. Yers crave immediate contact with friends no matter the time or the place. I discovered this one Friday night at about 10.30 p.m. Like many 30-somethings, I was at home in my pyjamas watching a DVD. Suddenly I was pulled away from Frodo and his heroic quest by the siren's call of an incoming text message. It was a message from Kristie, one of my Y girls, wanting to talk about the latest gossip from her first political conference. My immediate response was surprise at being contacted so late at night. But after a few moments I felt pleased, like I was one of the gang. This is what Generation Y do—too busy to see each other all the time, they rely on technology to keep up with each other's lives.

Communication technology—in the form of mobiles, email, online chat and of course texting—has become an indispensable tool for Gen-Yers in maintaining their friendship network (and their own status within it). Some prefer email and rarely use their mobile. Some are obsessed with text. Others use email sparingly because they rely on their phones. But everyone I spoke to used at least one of these technologies to organise their social life. Yers are texting each other in movie cinemas, on buses, in cafes and under the table in university tutorials. They use MSN chat to maintain contact with an old school mate who lives in another suburb or with a friend living overseas. They organise parties through email and text and send e-greetings instead of Christmas cards.

Email is particularly important for less mobile members of Generation Y, the office workers who face a computer screen all day. More important than email, mobiles generally and text specifically are absolute necessities. Whilst some members of Generation Y require a mobile phone for emergencies, paid work and volunteer-related activities, there is no doubt that it is first and foremost a social tool. For example, Anna describes her mobile as her 'main mode of communication with everyone'. Meg's mobile basically controls her social life. Kerry's mobile is her 'security blanket'.

When she is alone, she is comfortable and safe in the knowledge she can contact anyone at anytime. Very few members of Generation Y would like to think what living without a mobile would mean for their sense of what 18-year-old Curtis calls 'connectedness'.

Limited access to technology means a hampered social existence for Yers. Lawrence has a friend without a mobile and missing out on all the text messages means he is 'socially isolated, although he wouldn't think it'. If everyone else has a mobile phone and important social information is always communicated through text, then not having a mobile can send the average Yer into a neurotic frenzy. For example, if Sarah forgets her mobile, she is 'lost' and 'panicky'. Renee once forgot her mobile when she was interstate for three days and was so stressed she wanted to get it couriered to her.

So mobile phones have become a necessity and huge mobile-phone bills a reality. Phone bills are a big cause of financial difficulty for young consumers seeking financial help, with some members of Generation Y reporting thousands of dollars of mobile debt.[17] Whilst some young adults pay for their own phones, others have their parents foot the bill, an indication of just how essential mobiles have become. For some, their mobile bill is their biggest expense. For others, it is 'out of control'. When I interviewed Arya her mobile had been disconnected a few days earlier due to an unpaid bill totalling $1000. Living without it was 'killing' her! However, she didn't have to suffer for long. Two days after our interview, I got an email from Arya telling me her new mobile number.

The beneficiaries of all this—the telecommunications companies—have long recognised the close nexus between friendship and communication amongst young consumers, targeting the Y market not just as individuals but also as a tribe.[18] One TV ad for a phone that sends pictures shows a group of party girls messaging a house-bound friend encouraging her to come out and play. She dumps the boyfriend on the couch and goes out to dance with her girlfriends. Another ad tells you to 'Be One of the Others' by buying the latest phone with the latest gadgets. Advertising for mobiles is always a variation on a theme. New technology means being in the loop, up to date, part of the crowd. No technology (or old technology) means being left out, isolated, clueless.

The emphasis in all the talk about mobiles and text is on 'immediacy', being able to reach out to someone wherever you are and wherever they are. For Daney, text is 'all about real time—sending off something straightaway and getting an immediate response'. In the context of technology and Generation Y, immediacy and connection are one and the same. Mobiles are about 'what is going on now'. If you are disconnected, even for just a few days, you have a lot of catching up to do. Yers recognise that these technologies have changed the way they deal with time, shrinking it, injecting urgency into every social transaction. For example, Steve explains, 'Now the expectation is most people have a mobile phone, so you don't really worry about meeting people at a certain time.' While according to Sophie, this reliance on immediate contact has also made young people 'a lot more impatient'. She says 'If you need to meet someone and you can't contact him or her, it is really frustrating.' The Boomers were happy to wait a few days for a reply to a social phone call. Generation Y thinks ten minutes is too long to wait for a return text.

This impatience about the speed of connection with each other shows just how important the social network is to Generation Y, even though Yers like to see themselves as self-reliant and 'free agents'. Technology delivers what Generation Y is looking for in all relationships and pursuits—freedom and security. Your mobile phone gives you the security of immediate and constant contact with the freedom provided by mobility. Panic or frustration sets in when you are somehow separated from that constantly firing electronic network that maintains your social existence and friendship circle. You can opt in and out of this social world but technology gives you the up-to-date information that makes those choices possible.

Generation Y's emphasis on friendships above all other kinds of relationships is a defining element of that generation's mindset. In an insecure world of break-ups and sexual dramas, putting faith in a broader network of friends is a far safer bet than simply relying on your family or a relationship. This faith and trust in friendship may well be a result of changing labour market patterns for Yers' parents; because most Baby Boomers work, and work longer hours, their children have grown up spending more time with their friends than their family. It is certainly a consequence of Generation Y's experience with divorce and domestic turmoil. Seeing parents left without emotional back-up after a divorce sent the message to Yers that human pyramids are far sturdier structures than white picket fences. Related to this is that many members of Generation Y are postponing (or are pessimistic about) getting married and having children and so friendships become the long-term priority as well as a source of immediate security and entertainment. They make a commitment to their friends that they wouldn't dream of making to a job, a company, a brand, a political party or even a sexual partner.

This emphasis on friendship may diminish as members of Generation Y move into the future, eventually get married, have kids and reconnect with their biological family as they get older and move out of home. I have seen it happen with Gen-Xers who become closer to their mothers when they have a child of their own, spend more time with their father after he has a health scare and become closer to their siblings once they don't have to share the same bathroom. But the idea of the friendship circle as a 'second family' will persist as Generation Y gets older. They have a romantic vision of their friends that they don't have about family and sexual relationships, one that is too strong to be broken down easily. They place a particular value on friendships because they are relationships that provide a free and easy form of security in an insecure world. For Yers, friends are 'a security thing', 'a safety net' and 'a comfort zone'. In the middle of so much change friends are often the most stable resource you have. Understanding the emphasis Gen-Yers place on their friendship group is the key to understanding their attitudes on so many other issues—family, marriage, sex, relationships, work, consumerism and the future.

CHAPTER 3

Germaine Greer has left the *Big Brother* house

»

IN EARLY 2005, the iconic feminist Germaine Greer entered the *Big Brother* house in the United Kingdom, to live side by side with a B-grade crew of actors, pop stars and TV celebs. *Big Brother* is hugely successful with Y audiences around the world, largely because it successfully combines competition with voyeurism and audience interaction. *Celebrity Big Brother* adds another ingredient popular with the Y crowd— fame. In typical fashion, Greer got on well with the young and spunky male housemates, clashed with and condescended to some of the female housemates and attempted to stage a naked protest. She took over the cooking and complained about the state of the kitchen. In the end, Greer couldn't hack it. After four days she walked out, citing Big Brother's bullying tactics, 'physical and mental squalor' and her basic disapproval of reality TV.

The public reaction to Greer's surprise entry and even-greater-surprise exit was a mixture of bemusement and bewilderment. I was curious, however, about how *Big Brother*'s mostly young audience responded to the radical feminist turned Cambridge academic who had rubbished reality TV as undignified. A late January thread on the official *Big Brother* website reveals something of viewers' reactions (although, as with all chat sites, the age and gender of participants is difficult to determine). The verdict on Greer was mixed. 'Germaine needs a sense of humour to calm her down,' posted Andy Defra. 'She doesn't understand [*Big Brother*] and has a fixed opinion of it; she has become somewhat hysterical in her view.' 'I enjoyed Germaine while she was there,' posted CaptVimes, 'but she looks intent to continue in her attempts to stop something I enjoy watching.' 'Take the time to read the *Female Eunuch* to understand how far women have come today,' responded AngelHair. 'She has been wrongly cast as a man hater,' posted Heavenscentme. 'She seems more interested in humanity per se.' These comments from *Big Brother* enthusiasts demonstrate the diverse attitudes amongst Y men and women to feminism and its advocates. At their worst, feminists are man-haters, hysterical party-poopers with rigid ideas and no sense of fun. At their best, they are advocates for social justice for all, the drivers of a movement that has ensured women have come far and will continue to enjoy equality with men.

Attitudes amongst Y men and women about feminism are a logical consequence of that social movement's successes and failures. Y men and women take gender equality for granted. Y women were born and raised in the midst of a Girl Power culture, where being female was celebrated as something to be proud of.[1] They have been ingrained with the belief that they can do anything and be anything. In general, Y women know who they are and what they want. They believe, like 20-year-old arts graduate Meg, that a woman is 'as good as any man'. Y men grew up in the same environment, raised mostly by working, independent-minded mothers. This has ensured that a broad cross-section of younger men have grown up with basic feminist values and take equality between the sexes as a given.[2] As 19-year-old Laura says, in the eyes of Generation Y 'feminism is everywhere'. Female power, energy and success is reflected in popular music, movies and TV, at home in the reality of their mothers, in the form of their boss at work and in their teachers at high school and university. Their broader environment is one where men's monopoly on political and institutional power has been undermined and where the gendered organisation of paid work has been significantly disrupted. However, feminism's success has sowed the roots of its failure. Young men and women have internalised feminism to such an extent that many of them question its relevance as a social movement and a way of understanding the world.[3]

Generational queries about the continuing relevance of feminism started when Xers like me were at university. In 1996, journalist Kathy Bail compiled a collection of essays by young women about their attitudes to feminism. Entitled *DIY Feminism*, the book was in part a response to public criticisms of young women as reluctant and selfish beneficiaries of the Second Wave made by former femocrat and *Ms* editor Anne Summers. Why weren't our daughters embracing the women's movement and the label 'feminist', Summers asked?[4] In her introduction to *DIY Feminism*, Bail responded that young women were in fact living a new kind of feminist politics but one 'allied with a do-it-yourself style and philosophy characteristic of youth culture'.[5] This new politics rejected the 'woman as victim' strain of 1970s feminism along with the drab dress code, Stalinist manifestos and humourless sensibility. X women were tossing the loaded term 'feminist' (as associated with man-hatred and hairy legs) in favour of living a feminist politics that was diverse, creative, powerful and fun. This was feminism, but not as older feminists knew it.

Y women are much like their X sisters in their approach to feminism, in fact even more so. In her comparative research, academic Chilla Bulbeck found that only 55 per cent of young Australian women see feminism as relevant to their lives.[6] There are both proactive and reactive reasons for young women's disengagement with feminism and their aversion to using the word 'feminist' as a personal descriptor. Y women have reacted to the bad press which feminism, especially radical feminism, has attracted. They see gender relations as complex and shifting and are intolerant of generalisations about men and heterosexuality that permeate certain aspects of feminist debate. Some Y women see feminism as having 'gone too far', bringing about a sort of inequality. They are against what they call 'extreme feminism', which is sexist towards men. The vast majority of young women have so accepted the broad values of feminism—namely fairness and equality between the sexes—that they take issue with any kind of feminist thinking that calls for positive discrimination or denies anything to men.

There are also more positive reasons why many Gen Y women eschew the name 'feminist'. They have been brought up believing in their own independence and the opportunities available to them, particularly in education and the workplace. They refuse to see themselves as victims or in need of a political movement to help them succeed in life. Nov Thrupkaew argues that their 'do-it-yourself ethos' means young women don't feel like they need to be feminists in order to feel powerful and free.[7] Jackie is a glamorous and articulate 23-year-old, working in public relations. She believes that feminism is not as relevant to her and her peers as it was to previous generations because 'there is a lot more equality and opportunity now'. She believes 'The hard-core, radical kind of feminism' of twenty years ago doesn't seem to fit with this new picture. In general, these Y women (like many of their older X sisters) constitute the 'I'm not a feminist but…' generation. They believe that women should have the right to equality and fairness but don't class themselves as feminists and are in fact turned off by feminism's harder edges. Even Y girls who are politically radical tend to express any feminist beliefs within the context of other kinds of political activism. Many Y women activists involved in environmental or anti-globalisation work believe that in the process of this activism, they are disbursing feminist ideas.[8]

In fact, all the research and public comment on the reluctance of young women to align themselves with feminism can obscure the fact that a significant percentage still identify either as feminists or, more likely, with the goals and ideals of feminism. Many still recognise that whilst women have come a long way, we still live in a gendered world where discrimination, albeit subtle and intermittent, still exists. Of course within the group of Y women who still consider feminism relevant to their lives, there is a broad spectrum of feeling and opinion. There are young women like Karen who, at age 23, is still trying to figure out what feminism means to her. 'I know that it is important but I just can't seem to clearly define what it is,' Karen says. Many Y women honour the past achievements of feminism in bringing about social change. Miriam, a 24-year-old student from a Lebanese family, appreciates the 'great efforts' of feminists in increasing the rights of women and enhancing their value in society. She says 'I think the feminist movement has been crucial to the lives of women around the world and has been relevant to many women's, and men's, lives without them knowing it.' And it should never be forgotten that there is a small, definite group of Y women for whom being a feminist is vitally important. They are the distant echoes of a long feminist tradition in Australia, a dwindling but nevertheless committed group of Y women who, unlike the majority of their peers, still identify and draw strength from the movement.

Young women's disengagement with feminism is not hard to fathom. It is a movement that has benefited them to such an extent that some feel confident enough to question its continuing value. For those who still empathise with the movement, it provides a source of personal inspiration. But what about Y men?

In her research, Chilla Bulbeck found that only 23 per cent of young Australian men felt that feminism was relevant to them personally, a lower percentage than in similar countries like Canada and the United States. Y men join a good percentage of their Y sisters in believing that feminism is mostly redundant due to the significant achievements of women in the workforce. They see Y women as excelling at school and in their jobs, *living* feminism rather than needing it as a support system. In the light of this, Y men like 18-year-old Curtis believe that feminist initiatives like affirmative action are 'patronising' and 'breed too much male whining'. Like their female contemporaries, Y men feel that feminism has achieved much over the last three decades but now its work is mostly done.

Y men's reluctance to identify with feminism is understandable. Therapist and author Steve Biddulph argues that while feminism has been a necessary and important social movement for women, it 'does nothing for men'.[9] It offers a critique of male behaviour and attitudes but doesn't offer a way to be a new kind of man. Whilst Y men like Patrick, a 23-year-old law student, 'support the fundamental tenets of feminism', they are not sure it is directly relevant to their lives. Nevertheless, these young men have always been supportive of the feminist goals of gender equality and still remain so. That's because working, maybe even feminist, mothers raised the bulk of Y men. Young men like Blake 'grew up valuing the effort made by women to be independent and empowered'. He says 'It's part of a core belief I have. It's part of life now. It's becoming more and more integrated into the rest of society.' Because Y men were born and raised in a world already transformed by the feminist movement, gender equality is a no-brainer.

So amongst Generation Y there is a natural acceptance of gender equality as an important social goal, one that has practically been reached. Indeed, amongst Y girls there is a strong belief that for their generation of women, anything and everything is possible. This confidence, power and sense of infinite possibility are evidenced most strongly in popular culture. Since the early 1990s, TV and movies aimed at the Y market have been dominated by powerful 'girl heroes' like Xena the Warrior Princess, Buffy the Vampire Slayer, the Powderpuff Girls, the martial arts and spy chicks from *Dark Angel*, *Alias*, the movie remakes of *Charlie's Angels*, the list goes on. Sassy girls dominated popular music during the 1990s, the Spice Girls being a prime example of 'girl power' at its most obvious. In her book *Girl Heroes*, cultural studies academic Susan Hopkins argues that this 'new breed of pop heroine connects with girls who have grown up with more choices and more control over their lives than previous generations of women'.[10] They are 'competitive, combative and as capable of violence' as any Arnold Schwarzenegger type action hero.[11] This assertive and confident girl culture has also permeated women's magazines and literature aimed at young women (derisively referred to as 'chick lit').

This trend within popular culture has accompanied female success in education. As the first wave of Generation Y entered their final years of high school, Australian women made up nearly 57 per cent of all undergraduate entrants and nearly 49 per cent of post-graduate students.[12] Even prior to higher education, Y girls have been outperforming boys in high school, doing better on basic literacy tests and scoring higher in final-year exams.[13] In terms of employment, the general upward trend in the workforce participation of all women, which started in the late 1970s, shows no sign of subsiding. The proportion of women aged 15 and over that have a job hit an all-time high of nearly 61 per cent in early 2005.[14] Y girls see that they are doing better than their male contemporaries in these spheres. For example, personal assistant and aspiring fashion designer, Carolyn, says her girlfriends are actually surpassing her male friends 'big time' in terms of career success. All this supports the cultural messages that the sky is blue and the horizons limitless for Y women. Journalist Diana Bagnall observes that:

> ... quality and choice have been written into the school curriculum for more than two decades. Doors are wide open and girls take it as read that they can walk through them into good jobs, good money and the good life. Success has been mainstreamed for girls.[15]

Whilst overtaking their male counterparts in terms of 'good' behaviour, it seems that Y girls are matching the boys in 'bad' behaviour as well. In a newspaper article on girls behaving badly, Rose Herceg, Chief Executive of social forecasting company Pophouse, argues that 'the girls are able to misbehave as much as the boys' when it comes to sex and drug use. In Herceg's view, there is ample evidence that young women are behaving more like men in their attitudes to sexuality, picking up men, being more sexually assertive and pursuing short-term relationships.[16] Kristy, a 24-year-old, tells me she thinks women of her age 'have become much more aggressive in terms of picking up men and sex'. She says, 'I see some women going out to use men, who think that one-night stands are okay.' In terms of alcohol and drug use, girls are more than keeping up. There appears to be a growing range and prevalence of health-risk behaviours among young women. Twenty per cent of women aged

18–23 smoke regularly with another 12 per cent smoking occasionally. Seventy per cent of young women engage in 'binge drinking' at some time, with 19 per cent doing so on a weekly basis. Twice the number of teenage girls use drugs compared with their male counterparts.[17] It seems that for Y girls, gender norms have been destabilised to such an extent that swilling beer and cruising for a one-night stand is no longer the exclusive domain of young blokes.

What will dent young women's belief in what sociologist Valerie Walkerdine calls their own 'endless possibility'?[18] The answer is simple. Motherhood. Whilst Generation Y has been raised by independent, working mothers, it has almost certainly not been raised by house-husband fathers (or even fathers who fairly shared the household chores and child care with their spouse). For both X and Y, the message from their mothers has often been in conflict with the example of their fathers: as Hugh Mackay says of Boomer fathers, 'awareness [of domestic work] is one thing; action is another'.[19] Research seems to suggest that Y men and women, whilst content in their view that gender equality has been achieved and feminism's work is done, are actually headed for a protracted struggle when it comes to sharing domestic duties. Chilla Bulbeck's study found that 93 per cent of young Australian women believed that if both partners are working the same hours in paid work, they should share the housework and child care equally. However, only 70 per cent of young Australian men agreed. On the issue of role reversal—the idea of a breadwinning mother and a stay-at-home dad—86 per cent of young Australian women thought this was acceptable compared with 54 per cent of young Australian men.[20] With such vastly different attitudes, Y men and women are on a collision course. According to Chilla Bulbeck, 'boys don't look like changing and we are getting evidence that men are not.'[21]

In my own research, every Yer interviewed was asked how they thought children might change their life. The girls were forensic in their understanding of how being a mother and wife would transform their bodies, their working life and social life. For example, like all of her Y sisters, Jackie understands that 'having kids dramatically changes everything financially and socially'. Y girls want an equal partner at home but many are resigned to the fact they will have to compromise. Jenny believes she will have to fight with her future partner to achieve '70 per cent me, 30 per cent him', in terms of domestic responsibilities. She says 'Men generally don't have much of an idea about what's involved in domestic life. They do a little bit and assume that is a lot.' When the Y men I interviewed were confronted with the question about how children might change their life, their responses were vague and unsure. They often cited increased financial responsibility and not much else. The only Y men who understood what was involved in running a house and raising children were the more mature and aware young fathers.

Research on Y attitudes to domestic duties and child care shows that the gender landscape is changing, but slowly and unevenly. The new possibilities that have opened up for Y men are both exciting and confusing. The jury is still out about whether they are handling these changes well. Researchers who are focused on men's issues such as Steve Biddulph and Peter West have argued that boys are in trouble. Since the 1990s violence, antisocial behaviour, mental illness, unemployment and extraordinary rates of suicide amongst both boys and young men have made headlines and provoked public concern. Since that time, there has also been great government interest and some action on the issue of boys' performance in schools. Biddulph argues that 'school is a bad place for boys', where they 'do more poorly than girls in exams and have lower retention rates'.[22]

These problems exist in tension with evidence that young men's behaviour is altering. Y men have been born and raised in a world where alternatives to heterosexuality exist along with new images of masculinity. Within this context, hyperaggressive forms of masculinity are often presented as outdated, unhealthy and unjust. Indeed, Hugh Mackay believes that shifts in the gender landscape have allowed for a new group of men to emerge, what he calls 'the New Blokes'. According to Mackay, these are men from both X and Y who aren't SNAGs but aren't sexist pigs either. This significant block of young men combine the old-fashioned values of mateship and interest in sport and sex with the new values of a more sensitive and more relaxed approach to love and life, an interest in meaningful relationships and children. Mackay says the New Bloke is 'committed to work but knows there is more to life than 9–5'.[23] David Beckham and Jamie Oliver are examples of 'the New Bloke' at his most sexy and successful. Then there is the Metrosexual, often cited as a figure that proves this generation of men is breaking the macho mould. The Metrosexual is interested in personal grooming and style, shopping, decorating his home and entertaining his friends. He reads men's lifestyle magazines, goes to the gym, waxes his chest and watches his weight. Y guys like Ian Thorpe are Metrosexuals par excellence.

Whilst Y men are being offered some different ways of being a man, these new opportunities can be as confusing as they are liberating. Columnist Peter Holmes laments that in the new millennium a man must:

> . . . a) Appreciate where Naomi Wolf is coming from b) Look good in King Gee's and be able to design and build a new backyard in 48 hours with unfailingly enthusiastic mates c) Understand the difference between a bogey and an eagle d) Remember his feminine side while having the living daylights thumped out of him on the footy field e) Own at least one wok, one bottle of boutique olive oil, a pepper grinder and a Donna Hay cookbook f) Work until he's 75 years old to keep the bank at bay while developing a positive inner-self.[24]

Holmes's list of New Bloke/Old Bloke attributes highlights the fact that Y men are torn in various, often conflicting, directions by a world that hasn't yet made up its mind what it thinks a man should be. Tim, a thoughtful and funny 21-year-old, tells me that there are 'all sorts of conflicting pressures' on him as a Y man. He says 'Mum wants me to wear cardigans. My mates want me to stop wearing pink shirts. The girls that I hang out with want me to buy more pink shirts.'

In all this interest in men's grooming and cooking skills, the line between being a cool, hetero guy and being gay still has to be negotiated carefully by Y men. The premise of a popular show like *Queer Eye for the Straight Guy* is that a man can be well-dressed, polite, clean and stylish, whip up a mean soufflé and still be hetero. However, for Y men, the threat of being labelled gay still hangs in the locker room air. In their book about Australian boys, *Boys' Stuff*, Wayne Martino and Maria Pallotta-Chiarolli found that although young men wanted to look good and be physically strong, they still thought that 'a guy who works out at the gym ... and thinks he looks good in the mirror, probably ... has a tendency to be a fag or maybe a ponce'.[25] Laura, raised in Sydney's southern suburbs, agrees. She has a lot of 'surfie macho' male friends who would class a guy who goes to the gym and chooses his clothes carefully as 'a fag'.

There is even more evidence that just under the surface of these shifts in male identity, more conventional views remain fixed. For example, a letter published in *The Australian* in early 2005, entitled 'The great generation', lamented the fact that young Australian men broke down crying on meeting the last Fuzzy Wuzzy Angels who served their grand-fathers in the Kokoda Trail campaign in World War II. The author of the letter, N. Medcalf from Wyoming in New South Wales, concluded that 'In uncertain times it can be guaranteed that our country will need men, not over-aged adolescents who seem to need to broadcast their feelings publicly. I suggest that the young men of today leave the weeping to women.'[26]

This letter provoked much comment on the website www.insidepolitics.com.au. There was a mixed response, further evidence of how unclear the gender script is for Y men. 'Society better make up its God-damned mind what it wants—hard, stone-cold, wife-beating bastards or soft and gentle guys,' posted Pardus. 'Women have far more respect for a man who shows his feelings than the one who represses his angst only to blow his stack (or his brains out) at a later date,' posted Ms Gigabytes. Readinio, a 21-year-old man, agreed with the letter writer from Wyoming. In his post he described the young men of today as 'limp wristed cry-baby metrosexuals' who 'do not know how to deal with their own problems'.

In his book *Generations*, Hugh Mackay argued that the fundamental problem for Gen X guys was that their traditional roles had been challenged (primarily by feminism) without a new definition of masculinity having emerged.[27] The same cannot be said for Y men. Whereas the spirit and principles of feminism have infiltrated popular consciousness and allowed a girl power, 'I can do anything' culture to develop to empower Y women, the men's movement has not been influential enough to significantly alter societal views about what a man is and how he should look and behave. There have been changes in limited spheres. It is now socially acceptable for Y men to take care of their appearance and even enjoy shopping. But to some Y men these new 'freedoms' don't feel at all liberating. In the wake of second-wave feminism, masculinity has, according to Catharine Lumby, 'entered an age of profound uncertainty', from which it still hasn't emerged.[28] And so Y men are adrift in an environment where conventional masculinity had been subjected to substantial attack but where stereotypes about masculinity still prevail. The alternative ways to be a man that have developed in recent times—the New Bloke, the Metrosexual, the Queer-

Eyed Straight Guy—haven't yet got a firm enough foothold to fully displace the 'Man as Schwarzenegger' view of masculinity that Generation Y still retains deep in its psyche. In the eyes of Y, masculinity is still personified by famous football stars, action-film heroes and all-round tough guys (even though they understand these kinds of masculinities are unrealistic, oppressive and often brutal).

Y women have handled the changing gender environment to date with skill and confidence, boosted by the opportunities provided by the feminist movement and a popular culture that celebrates their power. Many Y women, bred to believe that anything is possible, will continue to succeed as long as they remain child-free. Their sense of infinite possibility will be tarnished by the realities of childbearing, child-rearing and domestic duties that their Y partners may well prove reluctant to share. Y boys will waver between the different models of being a man that society provides; this schizophrenic existence may well take its toll, even on the New Blokes and the Metrosexuals. Both Y men and women will hope they can avoid the domestic struggles over housework and gender roles they witnessed as children, struggles that resulted in divorce, unhappy marriages, resentment and emotional withdrawal. It seems Y girls in particular are willing to compromise and fight to ensure this doesn't happen.

In all of this, the relevance of both the women's movement *and* the men's movement is negligible. The spirit of feminism lives on and challenges for women in the home and the workplace exhibit a stubborn persistence. But the leaders of the Second Wave have struggled with the undeniably difficult task of updating feminist goals for the new generation. Boomer fathers haven't been much help either, in terms of providing their sons with new and satisfying models of masculinity or showing their daughters that men are capable of being equal partners in domestic and family life. Perhaps these fathers were too consumed with work. And, of course, women had more to gain from the women's movement than men did. Women got jobs, more money and power; men got to clean the toilet. However we look at it, the parent generation or the society it leads has yet to provide immediate and practical solutions to the Y generation's oncoming struggle with balancing work and family commitments. Until that happens, both Y men and women will feel as if the stormy gender seas will have to be navigated with their own compass.

CHAPTER 4

Mr Right or Mr Right Now?

»

BRITNEY SPEARS BLAZED on to the pop scene and into public consciousness right before the turn of the century. She was just 17. With her pigtails, Catholic schoolgirl uniform and glossy pink lips, she oozed precocious sexuality. In her video clip for her debut song 'Baby One More Time', she danced along school corridors backed up by her perky friends (male and female) who seemed positively bursting with confidence and team spirit. The 'Baby One More Time' video comes across as part pep rally, part teen love letter. In her early career, all of Britney's videos vibrate with Y energy, optimism and good clean fun. Gone are the X days of dark sexuality and angst. No more 'Tainted Love' or 'Careless Whisper'.

In a lengthy essay on Britney's appeal, American journalist Joe Lockard argues that a critical element of the early Britney image was her 'public chastity'.[1] In interview after interview, Britney spoke about her Baptist roots, her continued commitment to her religion and her decision to remain a virgin until marriage. She presented as a young woman saving herself for the right man, as Lockard observes, 'being sexy for the boys in the meantime'.[2] Despite her idolisation of Madonna, Britney was no Madonna replica.

Madonna, true to the tenor of her time, offered sex and was sure to go through with it (although she would have insisted on using a condom). Britney hinted at the possibility of sex, but with a disingenuous innocence. Her famous taught, tanned midriff was on constant display but Britney would have been appalled if you laid even a pinkie-finger on her honey-coloured belly button.

Britney is the ultimate American Y girl. Her early sexual persona reflects a central paradox at the heart of Y girl sexuality. The idealised Y girl is sexualised early, some-times before her teens, but must protest her status as a virgin. This kind of sexual innocence is a teasing deception. At 17, Britney may have been a virgin in a technical sense but her songs and dance moves were, according to Lockard, 'quintessentially anti-virginal'.[3] Her body, with its rumoured boob job and cheerleader curves, reflected anything but sexual purity. She was never that innocent. Now her image is tarnished, sullied by two marriages and the admission that her time with fellow Mouseketeer-turned-pop-prince Justin Timberlake involved more than just KFC and DVDs. She now appears in gossip magazines with bad skin and hair, pregnant, looking like the Louisiana trailer park girl she could have become had fame not waved its magic wand in her direction. Her 'brand value' is slowly disappearing, built as it was on a virgin status that has gone the way of the dodo.

Britney's public virginity (along with similar posturing by Y celebrities like Anna Kournikova, Jessica Simpson, Katie Holmes and Christina Aguilera) has been viewed by some commentators as evidence of a 'virgin pride' movement within Generation Y. In the late 1990s, the American media featured stories about 'virgin clubs' and 'vocal virgins'. Y girls and guys (many but not all of them involved in churches of all denominations) were signing 'True Love Waits' pledges and presenting them in Washington and other state capitals.[4] In TV shows and films aimed at the Y market, key characters celebrated their virginity—Dawson in *Dawson's Creek*, Donna in *Beverley Hills 90210*, the girls in *She's All That* and *10 Things I Hate About You*. (Compare this with the humiliation of Molly Ringwald's character in *The Breakfast Club* when she admits she is still a virgin or the excitement of Doogie Howser MD when he first has sex.) Whilst popular culture seems to increasingly sexualise the young, Howe and Strauss believe that young people themselves 'appear to be thinking harder than ever about the potentially grave consequences of sex'.[5] This supposed rethink about sex by Gen-Yers stands in stark opposition to the behaviour of their Boomer parents who, during their youth, experienced the full force of the sexual revolution. It also differs from the behaviour of Generation X. Teen sex in America peaked around 1990, when the tail end of Gen X was going through high school. Since Yers have entered puberty, sexual risk-taking and teen pregnancies are down from the levels to which Xers pushed them.[6]

Amongst the first wave of Generation Y, there are those who are willing to wait for the right time and the right person. Certainly many of these young people are religious or from ethnic backgrounds where premarital sex, especially for girls, is still considered a no-no. But others—both Y guys and girls—are simply waiting for 'the one'. For example, Brendon is 22 years old and a virgin. He plans to have sex only when he falls in love, which hasn't happened yet. He feels that his decision is atypical; his refusal to have sex has generated some negative reactions amongst his peers. 'There is a swing back to virginity, but I still believe that many people bow to the pressure to have sex fairly early,' Brendon says. Daniel is another Y guy who has remained a virgin by choice. He says that casual sex is fine for some, but it's not for him and most guys he knows would prefer to have a girlfriend rather than just a casual sex partner. 'The guys I know have lost their virginity with their girlfriends, not some random girl they met during Schoolies week,' Daniel says. 'It means a lot to guys too.' At 24, Miriam is still a virgin; she 'cherishes' the sexual experiences she has had so far, which have happened within the context of a serious relationship.

The position of these Yers is certainly not typical of this generation in its entirety—they are the resisters rather than the trendsetters. Because Gen-Yers are postponing marriage and intent on seeking adventure, choice and diversity in their lives, it is inevitable that they will spend their teens and early 20s engaged in various forms of sexual experimentation. For the majority of Generation Y this sexual experimentation starts in high school, between 14 and 16 years of age. The *Sex in Australia* report shows half of all young Australians have had or will have sex by the age of 16 with the majority commencing sexual activity by the end of high school.[7] This contrasts with Boomers, whose sexual activity commenced around the age of 18 or 19. There is also no doubt that Generation Y reached puberty earlier than previous generations, often before high school (hence the resonance and allure of schoolgirl Britney).[8] Despite teenage abstinence movements gaining momentum in Britain, the United States and even Australia,[9] the notion that the majority of young people will wait until marriage to be sexually active is akin to thinking that Elvis is still alive.

Most Yers describe their first and early sexual experiences as positive. A few are silent on the question, perhaps an indication of shame or embarrassment.[10] For others, sex didn't mean much until they found love. For example, Mary Jane didn't enjoy sex until she was in her first serious relationship. 'Everything before that was crap,' she says. 'Not negative, just a kind of nothingness.' Indeed, some Y girls express regret about these early experiences. Lee-Ann had sex when she was 14 but wishes she had waited until her late teens when she was 'mature enough'. Amongst Jenny and her friends there are definite regrets. Jenny says that there was 'an immense and unnecessary pressure to have sex' when they were 13 and 14. 'Why didn't we band together and put a stop to it? There was no question about giving into it. That was the culture.'

Generation Y's sense of sexual malaise is palpable. Amongst its members, there seems to be a nostalgic wish for an easier time when sex was something special. In her *Sydney Morning Herald* opinion piece on marriage, Amanda Fairweather, a recent high school graduate, describes the sex life of her peers:

> We have sex from a very young age and, unlike our grandparents, we don't wait for our soul mates or spouses . . . but basically sleep with whoever happens to be there and at least seems kind of into us at the time.[11]

Despite earlier sexual starting dates for most Yers, some elements of the sexual behaviour of young adults have remained constant since X and even Boomer days. Information about sex comes mostly from friends. Girls turn to magazines like *Dolly* and *Cleo*. Boys look at porn, hidden under mattresses and increasingly viewed online. Alcohol is almost always involved in those early experiences, especially with one-night stands. There is more pressure to have sex if you are in a social group where everyone is 'doing it' (or at least saying that they are). Popular girls with older or steady boyfriends are likely to be active earlier than their less popular, single counterparts. Despite the sexual and feminist revolutions, it is still easy for a girl to get a reputation for being a 'slut'—a sexual double standard is still strong, especially in the teen years.

But parents of Yers should sleep a little easier knowing that their children are now having safer sex than ever before. Contraceptive use at first intercourse increased to 90 per cent in the 2000s from less than 30 per cent in the 1950s. Young people, especially those living in urban areas, are the most likely amongst all demographics to regularly use condoms.[12] In their 2002 study of secondary students and sexual health, researchers at the Australian Centre in Sex, Health and Society found young people reported high levels of confidence in their ability to convince a partner to use condoms. Both Y girls and guys recognise the importance of good sexual health and responsibility. Meisha, an articulate medical student, tells me that she would definitely use protection all the way 'until you really know the guy'. But, as Arya reminds me, personal guidelines about contraceptive use can fall by the wayside 'as soon as you have a drink'.

Australian research indicates that straight Y guys and girls generally use condoms because they are concerned about unplanned pregnancy rather than HIV/AIDS and STD infection. In fact, it seems that the lessons about sexually transmitted diseases including HIV/AIDS will have to be re-emphasised to Generation Y. Since the 1980s, sexual health issues have become central to any discussion of sexual behaviour and attitudes. X was the first generation whose sexual education and early activity coincided with the emergence of HIV/AIDS into public consciousness. HIV/AIDS was recognised early on in Australia as an urgent public health issue. My generation remembers numerous public education campaigns on TV, in posters and in public toilets, including the famous ad featuring the Grim Reaper bowling at a collection of 'ordinary' people and knocking them down like tenpins. These ads were designed to shock and scare people into changing their sexual behaviour. It worked. In my generation's youth, fear of HIV/AIDS was everywhere and 'safe sex' became a common term.[13] An HIV/AIDS test became a rite of passage for a couple; going through the test together was a true sign of love and trust. But in the eyes of Generation Y, the Xers' fear of HIV/AIDS comes across as a quaint overreaction. Arya believes that there has been a backlash amongst her peers to this intense concern about HIV/AIDS amongst Xers. She says 'We got the other end of that fear in older people about AIDS. My generation is just not as conscious of AIDS.' Meisha agrees. She is much more worried about contracting STDs other than HIV/AIDS because these are 'more prevalent'. Whilst the level of knowledge about HIV/AIDS amongst young people is generally good, Generation Y is caught up in a general decline in understanding about its transmission. Knowledge about other STDs is poor, but improving, perhaps spurred on by the fact that a growing number of young people are catching sexually transmitted diseases like chlamydia and gonorrhoea.[14]

So Y sex is safer and occurs earlier. And it is also more varied. There is now more and more specific information about sex in sources like women's magazines, TV shows, advice media and the Internet.[15] As a consequence of this, Yers are aware from the start that there is more to sex than the missionary position. Y girls have grown up reading magazines like *Cleo* and *Cosmopolitan*, which since the 1990s have featured increasingly explicit articles on anal and oral sex, masturbation, sex games and toys. One of the latest and most popular sex toys amongst Generation Y is the mobile phone. Yers use technology to flirt and to initiate and maintain relationships. According to journalist Greg Thom, new 'techno-techniques' include 'SMS messages, camera phones, e-cards, singing phonegrams, virtual flowers and photo editing software'.[16] Pop mags have regular features about online dating and 'dirty text'. For example, Tony and his friends are big proponents of SMS dating. He says 'Instead of talking to a girl on the phone, you just SMS her. You have much more of a chance to sound witty and intelligent.'

On the whole, the diverse and varied sex lives of young people indicate that they, like Australians more generally, don't hold particularly conservative attitudes towards sex.[17] Most

Yers express a kind of laid-back, 'go with the flow' attitude to their sex lives. Jackie, single and 23, would prefer not to have a one-night stand 'but if it happens, whatever, it's not a big deal'. For Laura, it's just a question of 'liking someone enough and totally wanting to do it'. She sees no reason to be moralistic about it. This new generational openness to the infinite possibilities of sex is reflected in Y attitudes to a practice like oral sex. In contrast to previous generations, oral sex is now considered 'common practice' amongst young people. A young person's first experience with oral sex usually occurs before or during first intercourse (whereas their parents' first experience often occurred years after first inter-course). Maria and Kristie describe how their peers in the early years of high school used to go to the movies to 'pash' their boyfriends but that soon the pashing 'started going down'. There could be a number of reasons for this 'trend' in oral sex amongst Yers. Certainly oral sex is safer than inter-course and there is no threat of pregnancy. It seems that this generation, adopting Bill Clinton's logic, is less likely than older people to agree that oral sex constitutes having sex.[18] However, oral sex in this context is almost always one way, with Y girls going down on Y boys without the boys recip-rocating. Perhaps oral sex acts like a pressure valve in Y relationships initiated early. Not yet ready for intercourse, girls have been going down on guys to keep them satisfied whilst happily retaining their status as virgins.

The final, and in many ways most profound, change in the sexual attitudes and behaviours of Generation Y relates to sexual preference. Generation Y is the first generation to have grown up in a society and a culture where the issue of sexuality has been addressed openly. They have grown up watching Ellen come out on her sitcom, seeing the Gay and Lesbian Mardi Gras screened on public television and watching *Will & Grace* on prime time. Journalist Scott Ellis comments that after ignoring gay people for years, television suddenly discovered them in a big way in the late 1990s. Along with their older X siblings, Yers have made shows like *Queer Eye for the Straight Guy* a global phenomenon.[19] In the movies, music, gossip and magazines that Yers consume, sexuality is dealt with, debated and discussed without over-bearing moral judgment. Even Britney and Christina can kiss Madonna on MTV without raising too many Y eyebrows. This media visibility is complemented by the social and even family lives of Yers. As Martin points out, 'practically everyone knows someone who is gay'. Y urban dwellers socialise in clubs and pubs and attend dance parties where gay men and lesbians are visible and comfortable. Yers count gay people amongst their family, friendship circles and co-workers. Yers are more likely than Xers to have a gay parent or have been raised in a gay household.[20] Curtis says that living in metropolitan Australia, he is confronted with different kinds of sexuality every day, 'in the media, in the street and in cultural activities'.

Yers may even have gone to high school with other students who were comfortable and confident enough to come out. For Martin, coming out at a private boys' school was difficult but by the final year 'a lot of early hatred had faded away'. He says 'People just assumed I was gay but just dealt with it.' Once Yers entered university and the workplace, they almost certainly began circulating in an environment with gay people. Something that might have been contro-versial within the school context seemed unremarkable once Yers were operating in the wide world. One of Renee's best friends in high school was gay. Renee says that while a lesbian student at a Catholic high school was seriously gossip-worthy, she found that once she finished school 'no one cared'. 'You were out in the workforce, out of the sheltered school environment and there were heaps of gay people all around you,' she says. 'You learn to be accepting because you are exposed to it.'

Yers like Blake believe that the media's portrayal of same-sex relationships as 'a positive option' has meant his generation is more accepting of different sexualities. There is even a perception amongst some Yers that being gay is fash-ionable and cool, associated as it is with a lifestyle of dance parties, grooming products and free-flowing sexuality. The increased visibility of gay men and lesbians in our popular culture and in certain social contexts seems to have translated into broad political support for gays and lesbians amongst Generation Y. The Democrats Youth Poll has consistently found that a high number of young people believe gay, lesbian, bisexual and transgender people should have the same legal protection as heterosexuals.[21] Yers also believe their views about sexuality are more open-minded and tolerant than their parents. Brendon thinks that while older genera-tions haven't changed their mindset much in terms of sexuality, his generation has 'grown into tolerance'. Hannah agrees. Her peers are 'a lot more tolerant' than older people. She says that a number of her friends told her that they were gay and this hasn't changed their friendship in any way.

However, she adds 'My parents' opinions are a lot different.' This perception of tolerance is backed up by research. A 2001 Roy Morgan Poll found that while 36 per cent of all Australians believe that homosexuality is immoral, only 29 per cent of 14–24-year-olds felt that way. This tolerance of different sexualities fits with Yers' general acceptance of all lifestyle choices as equally valid. Whether it relates to sex, sexual preference, career or brand of sneaker, Yers put a premium on freedom of choice.[22]

But is tolerance the same as acceptance? Whilst the majority of Yers believe their generation is more tolerant of different sexualities, many wonder about the depth and breadth of this acceptance. For example, Jim thinks that his generation is 'more tolerant than accepting'. Steve believes that whilst people 'are far more accepting than they used to be', the majority of people his age 'don't look at gays and lesbians the same way they do straight people'. Tim finds that underneath the new acceptance of gay people, 'fears still exist'. He says 'Growing up, people still used terms like "fag" and "poof" to insult each other.' James believes that there is a slight difference between what people actually think and what they show on the outside.

> *Ninety-five per cent of people are accepting on the outside. But on the inside, there are many who are turned off on some level and think being gay is wrong. It may be the case that 50 per cent of people are totally accepting and the other 50 per cent aren't really accepting and don't understand it.*

Whilst gay and lesbian culture is, as urban-dweller David describes, 'part of the fabric, at least in our little corner of Australia', homophobic elements remain, even within this new open and accepting generation.

The shape of homophobia within Generation Y is very clear and relates in part to gender. It seems universally acknowledged that Y girls are more accepting of gay men and lesbians than Y guys. In her comparative work, Chilla Bulbeck found that 63 per cent of young Australian women believed same-sex relations are acceptable compared with 33 per cent of young Australian men.[23] This tolerance imbalance within Generation Y relates directly to the fact that the gender script has changed for women but not for men. Put simply, women pay a much smaller social price than men do for exploring their own feelings of same-sex attraction. As a consequence, Y girls seem much more willing to experiment with lesbianism. Y girls have read the stories in *Cleo* about lesbian chic.[24] They have watched as Marissa gave lesbianism a trial run on the popular television drama *The OC*. The university environment in particular is one where they can explore their sexual options with a measure of freedom. For example, Mary Jane had 'a couple of brief encounters' with girls in her early 20s. She says 'It was a great, fun, fresh experience. Those who were around at the time were not fazed.' Most girls that 23-year-old Jackie knows have kissed someone of the same sex.

Steve believes that Y girls are more capable of dabbling in lesbian relationships because they can always go back to the straight life without much controversy. 'Girls realise that they can try this experience for a while and then go back to men,' he says. 'I don't know many men who can do that. They realise they are gay and never go back.' Indeed, for Y guys the scenario is very different. In a very broad sense, being a real guy still means not being or acting gay. The fear of being labelled gay fuels continued homophobia, even banal forms of it, amongst Y guys. Tony's male friends might lust after gay women and fantasise about being a participant in some girl-on-girl action but this does nothing to diminish their fear of gay men. Tony reveals that:

> My guy friends can't get enough of lesbians! They don't understand it and they make jokes about it but they aren't scared of it because it doesn't affect them. One friend is so scared of gay men he would never go to a gay club. He thinks someone is going to make a move on him.

However, within this broader landscape of female tolerance/male intolerance, there are inevitable grey areas. There is evidence that some straight Y guys feel strong enough to challenge homophobia in their own social circle. In Tony's friendship group, there are a few boys who are homophobic. He says 'When they show signs of that we pay them out and give them shit. It is so old-fashioned and ridiculous.' Now that the awkward teen years are over, Daniel and his friends can say to each other that a guy is 'good-looking' whereas 'five years ago we couldn't'.

In addition to this gender dimension, tolerance of different sexualities has its own geography. Research has shown that 'less permissive' attitudes towards sexuality exist in regional and remote areas when compared with urban areas.[25] Indeed, most Yers recognise that whilst gay men and lesbians might feel largely accepted and comfortable in inner city areas and certain social circles, the situation is different outside these enclaves. Renee's family live in Redfern, a few minutes from the centre of Sydney. Her neighbours are two gay men who have custody of two little girls. She says 'My aunties and uncles who live in Parramatta visit us and freak. But to us they are just our neighbours. Where you live makes a big impact.' Jenny notices the difference between her performing arts school, located in Newtown on the city's fringe, where there are gay parents, teachers and students, and the northern beaches where she lives which is 'incredibly homophobic'. When Caroline moved from an inner city private school to a country school, she was shocked by the contrast. Her fellow students had 'homophobic views on a lot of things'. Caroline found 'I wasn't used to it. I thought it was something that didn't exist anymore.'

When the Boomers started the sexual revolution in the 1960s and 1970s, I bet they weren't thinking ahead to how it might impact on their treasured children. Boomers' sex lives started at a time when contraception was becoming widely available but sexual diseases like HIV/AIDS weren't an issue. They were rebelling against a straight-laced, religious and censorious society rather than hoping to fit into a sexually open and secular one. Many sexual radicals from the 1960s and 1970s now baulk at the images of overt teen sexuality in the video clips their kids watch on Saturday mornings. These parents have very little choice but to accept the sexual culture they helped create. Despite some evidence of 'virgin pride' amongst the more romantic and religious sections of Generation Y, there is ample evidence that this generation has become sexual and sexually active earlier than previous generations. The vast majority of Yers consider premarital sex acceptable.[26] All signs indicate that the majority won't be getting married until their 30s and so their sex lives outside marriage may span more than a decade. There is no doubt that early and regular exposure to sexual issues has made Generation Y more tolerant in a broader sense of all kinds of sexual expression and behaviour. This exposure has also helped make this generation more sexually aware and responsible. The sex lives of Yers will embrace a variety of partners and sexual experiences, maybe even same-sex experiences. Some may yearn for a time when sex was special and reserved for a serious relationship. But most of them—looking as always for a life of variety and experience—will take a less moralistic, more casual approach to sex. They are having fun with Mr Right Now but hoping they will find Mr Right at the end of it all.

CHAPTER 5

Maybe forever
»

ONE OF AUSTRALIA'S BIGGEST wedding websites is called www.i-do.com.au. Amidst the advertisements for cakes and flowers and photographers, there are sections offering advice about wedding etiquette, checklists for the big day and stories about weddings from hell. There is also a section entitled 'Young Hearts', devoted to stories about couples that have rebelled and decided to marry young. Most of these 'young hearts' were engaged in their late teens and married in their early 20s. Their stories are full of romantic joy and great expectations but also frustration and anger at other people's cynicism about their decision to commit early. Rebecca, who is 19 and engaged to Paul who is 25, found that the lack of support and backstabbing from those who were supposed to be her best friends was hurtful. She writes 'Like the rest of the young brides, if I hear "you're too young" once more, I'm going to scream!' Sarah is marrying her high school boyfriend Chris. She writes about not being taken seriously as a bride. 'When I go to bridal expos with my mum, a lot of people ask who's getting married. Mum loves it but I get a bit upset. If you're young and getting married, people think you're weird.' Lidia and Jonathon became engaged in their late teens. 'Everyone we met was against us getting married', writes Lidia. 'All we know is that we love each other very much and will make it work!' Reading these testimonials, it appears that marrying young is the new kind of forbidden love. Now that inter-class, inter-racial and gay unions have become commonplace, even passé, age has become the new marital taboo.

There is some anecdotal evidence around to support the theory of a recent upswing in young people getting married.[1] Y celebs like Britney Spears, Nicky Hilton, Nicole Ritchie, Katie Holmes and Christina Aguilera have recently married or got engaged (perhaps more for reasons of publicity than the desire to forge a long-term relationship). There is a widespread fascination with weddings amongst young girls, even those who don't see themselves getting married until their late 20s. Even inside the most sceptical Y women, like political staffer Arya, there is 'a little girl who thinks it would be so nice to be a princess for a day'. Certainly, wedding stories have increasingly become a favourite topic in the media, so much so that *Cosmopolitan*, a publication traditionally aimed at readers under 25, launched *Cosmo Bride* in 2003. The largest slice of the bridal title's readership, around 36 per cent, are women aged 18–25.[2] ·

For those Yers who have decided to tie the knot the reasons are varied. Certainly the majority of these do so because of religious devotion or ethnic background. But there are also those who have decided to marry young because they have recognised the potential problems with delaying these commitments until your 30s. For example, David is well educated, politically active and was engaged at

21. Even though David got married at the same age that his father was having kids, the engagement was a shock to people around him, including his best mate. David says:

He was really taken aback because he has a very different view about life phases and relationships. So much of the modern Australian experience is how much you are going to do and see before you settle down and become a grown-up. I think that's potentially a dangerous move. People risk not being young for their kids.

In this way the experience of Generation X is illustrative. Yers have seen a moral panic emerge around unhappy, childless and single 30-somethings. Many have older X relatives who are having difficulty either finding a mate or starting a family. Thoughts about a future of infertility, Internet dating and canned soup for one are enough to make early marriage seem like a good idea to these Yers.

However, despite the anecdotal evidence that young marriage is on the rise, few young Australians—only about 3.8 per cent—are currently living as a married couple.[3] All signs point to Generation Y continuing the trend, initiated by X, of 'postponing' marriage until the late 20s or early 30s. In the mid-1980s, the average age of marriage for Australian men was around 25 years and for Australian women 23 years. In 2001 it is now closer to 29 for Australian men and 27 for Australian women.[4] The majority of Yers nominate 30 as the magic age for marriage, the dawn of adult responsibility. Until then, they are content to continue a life of fun exploring bars, pubs and parties, experiencing different kinds of relationships, travelling, working and hanging out with friends. Even for those Yers who are committed to their partners, being in a 'serious' relationship doesn't necessarily mean wedding bells, even distant ones. Lawrence, 22 years old and the baby of a big, close-knit Catholic clan, sees a wife and kids in his future. He is reluctant to describe his long-term relationship as serious because he feels that seriousness in a relationship is 'hard to define these days'. He says 'I see myself as young so I don't see any relationship at this stage involving any life-long commitment.' He and his friends have reached the point where they are 'looking for a partner without looking for a long-term partner'. Lawrence can't see himself getting hitched for at least another decade.

Whilst Generation X's ongoing love and fertility difficulties have sent the message 'don't leave it too late' to Yers, only a few have responded by committing to marriage and children before 25. In fact, the more influential lesson, learned from their Boomer parents, has been the exact opposite, namely 'don't do it too soon'. Bernard Salt states that despite 'all their self-proclaimed radicalism', the majority of Boomers 'tied themselves to commitment early in life' and 'were married with a mortgage, children and a career by 25'.[5] Many lived to regret it, divorcing their spouses in middle age. Others stayed married, despite unhappiness and aggravation. Whether divorced or not, Boomer parents who regret taking on these early commitments have passed on a message to their kids—build a career, date different people, have sex, travel, live life before you settle down. Dissatisfied Boomer mothers in particular urged their girls to claim their independence before getting hitched. For example, Hannah's mum was married at 18. Hannah was content to have a child at 18 but she considers herself too young to get married because of her mother's experience. 'Mum always told me eighteen is too young to get married,' Hannah says. 'Even though she is happy, she regrets it now. She is always telling me go out and have a life before marriage.'

In this way, Yers are squeezed between the regrets of the parent and previous generations. In her opinion piece on young people and marriage, Amanda Fairweather writes that her generation 'has seen the deep-set lines of sadness and the unfulfilled look in the faces of both those women with the shoulder-padded business suits and the bored housewives in the floral dresses'.[6] However, whilst some Yers worry about missing out on marriage and parenthood like many Xers, they are more concerned about avoiding the mistakes of their parents.

It's no surprise to learn that Y attitudes to marriage are shaped primarily by the example of their parents. Yers were born and raised in an environment where divorce was no longer rare or the subject of social disapproval. They were raised in families touched by divorce or had close friends whose parents had split up. In the years between 1986 and 2001 (the Yers' child and teen years) the number of divorcees in Australia almost doubled from 0.6 million to 1.1 million.[7] Inevitably this period saw the number of one-parent families in Australia increase by 53 per cent, in contrast to the number of two-parent families with children that increased by only 3 per cent. The number of divorces granted in 2001 was the highest in the past twenty years.[8] Yers have grown up dealing with the aftermath of broken Boomer fairytales and the sometimes tricky web of family and living arrangements these ruptures create. Remarriage, de facto relationships, blended families and multiple-family homes—Yers are familiar with all these arrangements.

This early exposure and experience with divorce has had a mixed effect on Generation Y. On one level, it has ingrained in Yers a realisation that marriage is an imperfect institution. In her research on young adults who experienced parental divorce as children or teenagers, psychologist Claire Cartwright found her subjects had problems in their own intimate relationships, including doubting their own ability to sustain a long-term relationship, a lack of trust in potential partners, fear of divorce and cynicism about marriage.[9] Claire, a 24-year-old university student, believes that marriage is a problematic issue for her generation because many Yers have divorced or separated parents. 'I think that makes us more critical of marriage, questioning the meaning of marriage, how it affects our sense of self and the way that divorce can create so many traumas, especially for children,' Claire says. 'We know that marriage may not be forever.' Claire wants to get married and make it last. However, her parents' experience has made her aware of the realities of sustaining a union in the face of work and money pressures:

> *I am not naïve enough to believe that a marriage will weather all storms. I worry so much about the importance of money in our lives and I think that so many marriages have ended because of financial issues. Love cannot always transcend economic realities. In the case of my parents, when their business was lost, they*

separated. They have been on and off ever since. I know that I don't want a marriage like this.

While there are many stories like Claire's amongst Gen-Yers, it is often those whose parents are unhappy but remain together who seem most scarred by the marriage experience.[10] Sophie's parents are together but are 'not happy by any means'. Recently out of a long-term relationship, Sophie is pessimistic about her capacity for commitment. She says 'My mum has been talking about leaving my dad for the last ten years. Just considering my family background, I probably will end up getting divorced but by no means do I wish it to occur.

However, Generation Y's familiarity with divorce has had another, less obvious side effect than the pessimism about eternal love expressed by Sophie. Some Yers have lived with the pain and difficulties divorce creates or witnessed the unhappiness caused when two people who should be divorced stay together. Those Yers whose parents have remained happily married are keenly aware that this is a great and enviable achievement. Either way, the majority of Yers are determined either to emulate the success or avoid the failure of their parents. The majority believe in marriage as an institution, even revere it. Young mum Maddy believes that 'People get married because they think it is just as easy to get a divorce. I don't want that. When I get married, it will be a life commitment.' Kristy also believes that 'marriage is not to be taken lightly and rushed into for the hell of it. It's for life.' Her friend, of the same age, married after a seven-year relationship then divorced a year later. Kristy says 'You have to be 100 per cent sure you want to commit to that person for the rest of your life.

This sincere belief in the importance of marriage isn't just held by Y women, though they may be more vocal about it. Tim, a young Y father, believes 'marriage is wonderful'. He says 'There is no greater honour than to commit completely to another. Marriage is much more enjoyable, comfortable and stress-free than single-ness.'

In light of their deep commitment to marriage as an institution, how do Yers believe they can avoid the mistakes of their elders? Again, their parents' experience guides their present course. Unlike their parents, the majority of Yers are reserving their 20s for having fun and experiencing life. As a single 23-year-old, marriage seems a world away to Patrick. He says 'At this stage I want to chase life experience, not comfort, stability and security. I can't see myself making such a commitment in the short to medium term.' Meg agrees, saying, 'Boys and girls just want to have fun while they are young, so living out of home and doing your own thing is important.' For Y boys in particular 'fun' in your 20s is about sexual experience. Curtis, bluntly assessing why men his age postpone marriage until their late 20s, says 'Some men of my generation harbour aspirations of marrying for good, but this is more likely to be when they want to stop sleeping around.' Y girls too have identified sex as a major priority for Y guys. Diana, 20 years old and a mother of three children, believes men her age 'would probably be terrified of marriage because they love being able to sleep with whoever whenever'. Caroline agrees. 'A lot of my guy friends do want to settle down but much later on. Now they just want to sleep with a lot of girls and have fun.'

Another current priority, which is hard to reconcile with marriage and kids, is travel. Yers want to study, live and work overseas as well as spend extended periods of time back-packing. Whether travelling with a partner or leaving them at home, an exclusive relationship seems to be at odds with the promise of freedom and adventure which globetrotting offers. For the more serious-minded Yers, study and training and establishing a career and a financial base are important prerequisites to a more settled life. Dace, a 25-year-old from Vancouver, believes that people his age are getting married later because they want to be 'more established in terms of money and a career'.[11] The price of a house and family is so much more than it was for their Boomer parents and so Yers recognise that it might take their entire 20s before they can commit to mortgage and childcare payments. Even those Yers who married before 25 recognise that other life priorities need to be dealt with before tying the knot. 'Young Hearts' Sean and Amy write of their struggles to maintain their relation-ship through her university studies, his apprenticeship and her study trip to Africa. After all this personal growth, they can now live together and plan their October wedding.

In all this sex, travel, work and study, Yers are hoping to understand themselves and establish a lasting identity in the process. This is a particular priority for girls. The feminist movement has gradually altered what marriage means for women. It has been transformed from a restrictive institu-tion to one in which a woman can maintain her identity and independence. Nevertheless, Y women have heeded the call of their mothers to get the most out of life before marriage. And so 'finding yourself' and establishing your credentials as an individual is a particularly important goal for Y girls. For example, Meg wants to get married in her late 20s but until then 'living independently' is what is important to her. Y women like Meg realise they have more options in their 20s than just marriage and children. As young women, they are career focused and intent on establishing financial security as well as a strong social network. As journalist Adele Horin writes in her article most young women 'wouldn't dream of living off a man even while living with him'.[12] It's not surprising then that, for Y girls, the ideal form of marriage is one where two people find security in their commitment to each other without losing that sense of self which they spent their 20s cultivating. As Hannah sees it, marriage should be about 'two people living a life together but not losing their identity, working as one but remaining individuals'.

Even for those Yers who have decided to marry early, their own independence and identity remain a priority. Renee is from a Christian Lebanese background and is a successful HR manager in a big company. She had been engaged once, to a boy from a similar ethnic background, but she broke off the engagement. Renee explains that their different incomes was an issue—after studying, she had 'a really good job but he was still trying to find his bearings'. She says 'I started seeing a part of our culture I didn't like, that male domination stuff. I thought, this is not me. I don't want to be confined in terms of how far I can go with my job.' Renee did marry, but her husband is Australian, older than her and very supportive of her career.

Even for those Yers who have experienced fun, travel and personal fulfilment, marriage seems less necessary when cohabitation is a genuine and socially acceptable option. If a Y relationship becomes serious, it is far more likely to lead to cohabitation than marriage. In 2002, 6.8 per cent of all young people were living in de facto relationships, almost double the number who were living as married couples.[13] Cohabitation amongst couples prior to marriage has increased from 44.6 per cent in 1986 to 72 per cent in 2001.[14] Cohabitation amongst Yers takes different forms and emerges for different reasons. Whilst two out of three couples who live together eventually marry, not all Yers see cohabitation as the last step before the altar.[15] In some cases, living together is more about economic necessity and convenience than it is an indication of a permanent commitment. Adele Horin comments that for young Australians in their early 20s, it is often real estate prices rather than romance that determines their living arrangements. For these couples, their decision to share a bed and the rent is 'part convenience, part love, part sex'. Horin observes that 'They are together but words like "our future" or "next year" don't crop up. They have big plans for their lives but they are not shared plans.'[16]

Then there are those Yers living together who are happy with the status quo and see no great reason to formalise it. For example, once he has the money set aside, post-graduate student Liam will move in with his long-term girlfriend. They have decided to live together rather than get married because neither of them believes that marriage would change their relationship. Liam says:

> I don't see marriage as something that is either worthwhile or not worthwhile in the times that we live in. It doesn't matter one way or another. We are both quite happy continuing in a de facto relationship. I see it continuing for a long time.

Even for those Yers who are headed towards the altar, living together is an important precursor to marriage. Cohabitation is a prerequisite to marriage because Yers want to trial-run their relationships under close-quarter conditions to help ensure its success. Again, the rise in cohabitation before marriage is not a symptom of Yers' disregard for marriage but their intense concern about getting it right. Meg thinks it is 'vital to live with someone before you get married to truly find out what they are like'. Blake believes living together is 'a must do' if you take marriage seriously. Lee-Ann already owns a house with her de facto. She says 'At first I thought I would probably have preferred to be married.' However, Lee-Ann now feels that being de facto 'is the best thing'. 'There is too much divorce in the world,' she says. Karen recognises there is a real generational difference in terms of cohabitation. She says 'My parents and their generation think that if you're going to live together, why not get married?' Whereas Yers think that if you are going to get married, you should live together first.

Yers want to live life to the full before marriage, finding out all they can about themselves in the process. When they do meet someone they are serious about, they are determined to test-drive the relationship under all kinds of conditions— travel, sickness, sharing living space and domestic chores—before making the final commitment. Many of them seem to be consumed with fears about making a mistake. For example, Lawrence plans to 'experience different people and travel the world' in his 20s. He says 'The last thing you want to do is get married and have regrets.' Sasha is a 25-year-old consultant from the United Kingdom. Her parents are still together but they went through 'a rocky patch' when she was younger. Sasha wants to get married and she 'never wants to get divorced'. Her fears about making a marriage mistake manifest themselves in her dreams:

> For about three or four years now, I have had dreams about getting ready for a wedding and walking down the aisle and sometimes seeing the face of the person at the end and sometimes not. And every time having the most terrible, gut-wrenching feeling that this is the wrong person. That I can't marry them and I'm terrified about what I am going to do about it. I feel trapped. I am not someone who just wants to get married for the sake of it. I'd have to be totally sure.

There is no doubt that Yers' intense concerns about marrying the right person is evidence of their deep commitment to marriage as an institution. As Y writer and webzine editor Rachel Hills comments, whilst 'Britney and J-Lo might be OK with fly-by-night marriages and quickie divorces . . . if most young people are going to choose to get married, they want to choose right.'[17] Many of them have witnessed the mistakes and regrets of their parents (whether separated or still together) and they are determined not to repeat them. They see life without divorce as an achievement,[18] up there with big job promotions and property acquisition. But all this anxiousness about mistakes and regrets, the shadows cast by their parents' failures or the desire to live up to their success, exerts a unique pressure on Y relationships. A report in a recent edition of the journal *Family Matters* found that whilst 'Australia's young are strongly pro-marriage', many are unlikely to achieve it because they are 'too cautious and choosy'.[19] In their need to ensure they get it right, Yers are searching for guarantees that cannot be found. Some, paralysed by worries about making the wrong choice, might opt to continue the life of freedom and self-fulfilment of their 20s into their 30s and beyond. But most will hope that the right person will come along around the age of 30, sometime between too early and too late.

CHAPTER 6

A job for life

»

IN EARLY 2004, I arranged to meet Laura, an ex-student of mine, to interview her for this book. We met at Central Station and settled into a quiet cafe nearby to talk. When I met Laura she was at a loss about what to do with her life. She came across as fiercely bright and opinionated in class but it was clear that she wasn't enthusiastic about being at university. She was expected to be there rather than wanted to be there. Laura grew up in the Sutherland Shire, an hour from the centre of Sydney. Her mother is a semiretired primary school teacher. Her father was a manager of a medium-sized company, but was fired a few years earlier for refusing to move interstate when the company relocated. Laura excelled academically at high school. Looking back on it now, she wished she had taken a year off between school and university in order to travel. Annoyed with her own lack of interest and drive, Laura deferred her university degree for a year. She spent a few weeks in the Army Reserve but dropped out due to injury and her tendency to question orders. When we had lunch together, she was working three days a week as a waitress. If she had her choice of any job in the world, it would be a theatre director. However, enrolling in the necessary course would mean moving closer to the city and away from family and friends. Some of Laura's friends are doing commerce degrees 'because there is a job at the end'. Others are doing the course that interests them with 'no idea what the job at the end of that will be'. Whilst she doesn't worry too much about job security, she was worried enough to choose psychology over theatre when she first applied for university entrance.

Laura's attitude to work and career is typical Y. Yers are highly educated and value institutionalised learning; a generation that kick-started positive trends in educational achievement, especially for girls.[1] Well before they entered high school, many Yers were subject to extreme pressure to perform at school.[2] As Howe and Strauss found they are used to 'the bar is moving, ever upward' when it comes to academic standards.[3] However, once out of the high school system and road-testing their independence, many have lost their previous focus and drive. They find themselves struggling to find meaning and purpose when it comes to work and career. They want to learn, succeed and earn money to fuel their high-level consumption habits. However, they value a balanced life. They want to feel passionate about what they do. But until they find their calling, many are content to settle for a series of 'McJobs'[4] to fund a life of fun, travel and time with friends. Job insecurity isn't that big a deal. Most know there are plenty of 'crap jobs' out there they can get. A bigger concern is finding the 'dream job', one that provides financial security *and* personal fulfilment.

The statistics on young people and employment paint a fairly grim picture of the career and financial prospects for Laura and her peers. Labour force figures show that youth unemployment remains high, with at least one in five young people out of work.[5] Since 1993 there has been a significant decline in apprenticeship places in the major trade occupations.[6] Previously there was a close nexus between unemployment and lack of education and training. Not so for Yers (or indeed their X counterparts). Educated Yers, especially those who have come out of tertiary education rather than the trades, are facing a highly competitive job market. In the United States, the college classes of 2003 graduated 'into the nation's worst hiring slump in 20 years', with only about 15 per cent leaving school with jobs waiting for them.[7] The cluey Yers, like Jim, recognise this. A politics undergrad at a prestigious university, Jim is worried about his job future. He says 'I'm doing an arts degree, and some of the brightest graduates I know are finding it impossible to get work seven months after finishing university.' Claire feels the same way. She is unemployed and trying to finish an Honours degree. 'I worry constantly about money and not having a job,' Claire says. 'Potential employers still have a dismissive attitude towards arts degree holders. I worry I won't get a job on an arts degree alone.'

Many university graduates face the terrible realisation that after years of expensive study, they may well be applying for jobs they could have landed *without* a university degree. Changes in our economy and industrial base have created a job climate where there will be no shortage of low-wage jobs around. But interesting and secure employment for everyone coming out of university is a thing of the past.

In the face of these facts, the line spun to Generation

Y by parents, teachers and broader society—'work hard, do well at school and you will have a successful career'—is exposed as a pernicious lie, up there with 'stop it or you will go blind'. The certain belief in the power of education as the path to success was passed from Boomer parents to their offspring at an early age. Investment in Y educational achievement started almost in the crib. Competition for the best schools, universities, courses and marks has driven even low-income parents to pour all of their resources into their children's education. For most Yers, even those with parents on low incomes, the move from high school to further education and training seemed non-negotiable. In the movie *Orange County*, the overprotective mother, played by Catherine O'Hara, asks her ambitious son: 'Why do you have to do go to college?' Her son, played by Colin Hanks, screams back at her, 'Because that's what you do after high school!' Nineteen-year-old Curtis believes there is an 'assumption amongst his peers that tertiary education is the norm' and that it will lead to 'manifestly better job prospects'. Claire agrees, arguing that parents' personal investment in their children's academic success fuels this assumption:

> *My family always expected I would go to university. I went to a private school and everyone there just took it for granted that we would do the HSC and then a degree at university. It would have been seen as a sign of failure or lack of ambition not to go on to tertiary education. Parents see having children at university as a status symbol.*

Once out of high school and into higher education, the pressure to perform doesn't stop. University was once a place to learn but also where you could skip class to attend meetings, see films and generally revel in campus culture. Almost extinguished is the romantic view of university as a place to broaden your mind, find yourself and dabble in radical politics. It is now a place to get qualified for a job that helps pay off education debts as soon as possible. As David Brooks observes in relation to elite college students in the United States, 'more kids are entering [university] in a prudential frame of mind' and 'see their education as a means to an end'.[8] This pressure to get through and get qualified a.s.a.p. is exacerbated by the fact that most university students have to work as well as study full-time in order to live.[9] Jenny's parents expected her to go to university because 'they had an amazing time there'. She believes that 'you could basically stay there as long as you wanted' in those days. 'My dad was there for six years doing a basic undergraduate degree,' Jenny says. 'You can't do that now. Rent is so high and you are acutely aware that you are paying for your education. There wasn't much social life on campus when I was studying.' Scott is involved in campus politics and postgraduate study. He says:

> People just want to get in and get their degree so they can get working. They don't have time to worry about much else because their families are investing so much money in their education. Even for an arts degree, your HECS debt is quite a burden coming out of your pay packet every fortnight.

After years of educational achievement and investment, many Yers are graduating into an environment where there are more graduates than quality jobs. Yers are also leaving university with big HECS debts which many will struggle to pay off quickly. One in ten Australian students graduated from university in 2004 with more than $40 000 in debt.[10] Most graduate with debts between $20 000 and $30 000 (a sum usually reserved for a house deposit). Whilst current levels of HECS debt haven't retarded enrolment rates, HECS debt does constitute a real handicap for Yers entering the workforce, at a time when they may want to establish a stronger and more independent financial base.[11]

Paying back a big HECS debt is not the only financial hurdle Yers, even fully employed ones, face. The question of living expenses, in particular the cost of housing, is an even bigger concern. Rent in urban areas where the majority of young people live, work and socialise is high. Housing prices are even more prohibitive.[12] HECS debts and the cost of Y-style living combine to prevent the majority of young people from saving any money, let alone enough for a house deposit. For example, Daney believes he is 'stuffed' financially unless he ditches his union organiser job for a law career. He says 'Even if I managed to scrape up a deposit for a house, I wouldn't be able to make the repayments because my HECS debt takes a chunk out of my income.' Whilst the Australian dream of owning your own home is still 'firmly entrenched' in the Australian psyche, home ownership has fallen among young people.[13] The crisis in housing affordability is so acute than many Yers nominate it as a key political concern amongst their age group. For example, Antony believes that his peers are 'beginning to doubt whether owning your own home is a possibility'. Jackie and her friends all worry that if they stay in Sydney, they will never be able to afford a house. 'A lot of people my age talk and worry about that,' she says. Arya agrees that the toughest issues facing her generation are 'whether or not we can afford to survive the next twenty years and get those things we have dreamed of like a good career and a good home in a good area'.

It is true that some Yers could afford property. But the only houses in financial reach are on the urban periphery, away from established friendship networks and familiar places. For most, that's too great a price to pay for four walls and a roof. Kristy and James are in their mid-20s and live in the city. Both travelled after study then settled into jobs in hotel administration and finance respectively. Whilst they are concerned about home ownership, they aren't prepared to sacrifice everything for a place of their own. 'No one really can afford to buy a home or wants to put that much commitment into a mortgage,' says James. 'People our age want to live where they want to live.' Like Yers, Xers also feared the depressing effects of home ownership. Coupland observes that:

> *When someone tells you they've just bought a house, they might as well tell you they no longer have a personality. You can immediately assume so many things: that they're locked into jobs they hate; that they're broke; that they spend every night watching videos; that they're fifteen pounds overweight; that they no longer listen to new ideas.*[14]

Starting out is always a hard task. But for Yers, moving out of home and establishing true financial independence may take more than a decade after graduation. Until then they will zigzag from share accommodation to parental hearth. Indeed, Yers are consistently relying on family to keep them from financial hardship and provide a roof over their heads. The majority of young people aged 15 to 24 live at home, with nearly 46 per cent of 20–24-year-olds still with their parents.[15] Successive Democrats Youth Polls have shown that the main source of income for more than half the population of young people is their family, well above employment, social security or youth allowance.[16] Even if Yers leave the family home for a period, many return, 'boomeranging' sometimes again and again, due to financial or relationship difficulties. For example, Liam left home after high school and moved in with friends while he was working as a junior clerk in an insurance agency. He had fun, but didn't manage to save, so when he started his postgraduate degree he moved back in with his parents. 'I just couldn't work and study at the same time,' he says.

This situation creates a strange double bind. The Boomers were in the right place at the right time in terms of the property market, buying up big when paying a mortgage was cheaper than renting. Having locked up the housing market, many have chosen (or been forced) to continue to support their young adult children, providing them with low-cost rent or rent-free accommodation, lending them the deposit for a house, or leaving the family home to them entirely and moving away. But the stress on Boomers will mount as they near retirement and need to save more money. (Students aged 18–25 still living at home are the most expensive age group to support, costing approximately $322 each per week in 2002.)[17] This may well frustrate and disadvantage Yers still dependent on their parents. Used to the high living standards of their childhood, many will struggle with what Coupland calls 'homeowner envy',[18] exacerbated by current inequalities in income and employment in the workforce.[19]

In the face of all this—an insecure job market, the diminished value of a university degree, HECS debts and ridiculous housing prices—how have Yers reacted? They have made realistic adjustments to the world's instability[20] by taking unstable employment as a given and adopting a self-reliant, survival-of-the-fittest attitude to career success.[21] Most are repelled by the idea of 'a job for life', the kind of employment stability as understood by their parents and grandparents. In fact, the majority would view staying with the same company or same job for more than a decade as the equivalent of a death sentence. Many Yers enjoy the opportunities and sense of freedom an unsure career path can provide. For 23-year-old law clerk Patrick, thinking about career plans at his age makes him 'grimace'. He says 'Who can know what might happen?'

When asked where they would like to be in their career in two or three years' time, Yers talk about the same role in a different company, the same company in a different country or a different career altogether. Human resources expert Catherine Allen observes that even the best-educated Yers have changed jobs or careers in the past five years. In her article on generations at work, she writes 'They jump from one job to another rather than climb a ladder [and] they do not stay in jobs they dislike.'[22] Yers are particularly enthused about jobs that provide the opportunity to travel—like Trudi, a librarian, whose dream job would be to administer a library on a cruise ship. Most Yers want to integrate travel into their working lives. That can mean taking jobs that provide opportunities overseas, working overseas for a couple of years or using brief periods of work to fund backpacking trips.[23]

This professional wanderlust contributes to Yers' relative lack of concern about job security.[24] Whilst successive Democrats Youth Polls have found that only half of their respondents felt they had job security, most are unfazed about this situation because they know there is always unskilled work available to them. They also know that at present it is an employee's market, especially if you aren't too picky about the kind of job you want. For example, Tony has been employed since he was old enough to have a job. He has worked in a butcher shop, as a delivery driver for a Thai restaurant and as a kitchen hand at a racecourse. In his opinion, 'Being unemployed is not a possibility.' He says 'I will just take what's on offer even if it is crap—and it usually is. I am never concerned about unemployment.'

So Yers have reworked employment insecurity into vocational freedom and the opportunity to travel, experience new workplaces, expand skills and stave off boredom. Above all else, they value flexibility and diversity in their working lives. Researcher Rosemary Herceg found that the majority of young people 'talk about a way of working that is smarter rather than harder'. She says 'They speak about things like working from home, marketing their ideas rather than their time, and moving away from the daily 9–5 grind.'[25] In order to manage Generation Y workers effectively and get the most out of this highly educated cohort, employers are going to have to rethink their management practices. They are going to have to embrace, rather than grudgingly allow, the whole range of flexible work options available—job sharing, quality part-time work, flexible hours, working from home, and all sorts of education, training and travel opportunities. They are going to have to keep a long leash on Generation Y employees or risk losing them altogether.[26]

This lack of a deeper connection to the world of work is the Yers' reaction to the broader economic climate but is also a consequence of their experiences during childhood. Most Yers were born in the 1980s, an era of downsizing, de-regulation and leaner, meaner corporations. A time when both public and private institutions hardly thought twice about firing hundreds of loyal employees for the sake of a profit margin. Yers like Laura have seen their hardworking parents dismissed from their jobs after years of service. Generation Y learned a number of lessons from these early experiences. Don't expect much or trust big institutions, corporate or otherwise. But more profoundly, don't invest too much in your job because your bosses aren't that invested in you. It has become a truism that Yers lack a deep commitment to their current job, lack long-term loyalty to their employer and have a tendency to change employers frequently.[27]

The example of their parents also taught Yers to value life outside work. In an article on young people and overtime, 20-something Alan Mascaredbhas describes his father as 'an overworked marketing executive' who died in a freak accident during an office picnic. Mascaredbhas was nine at the time. 'Probably not the first person to give his life for his job but it left me determined not to repeat the achievement,' he writes.[28] Yers are living witnesses to the personal cost of their parents' workaholism—broken marriages, absentee parenting, stress-related illnesses—and have been left disillusioned and determined to achieve a balance in their own lives. Generation Y expert Mark McCrindle argues that young people 'do not live to work, rather, they work to live'. McCrindle says they value jobs that 'provide the income to do what they want to'—have fun, travel and spend.[29] But they also want to achieve the work/life balance that still eludes their parents. Many of them are therefore turning down jobs or overtime that spills over into their social time, regardless of the pay on offer.[30]

If Y desires to achieve a balanced life are strong enough and can be sustained into homeownership and parenthood, this generation may yet transform the world of work. Work/life balance issues are a priority for both Y guys and girls. Again, the experience of their parents has proven illustrative. Y girls were born during a decade of 'The Superwoman'. This idea (a perversion of the feminist message about female empowerment) was that your average woman could maintain a career, a relationship, raise multiple children and still manage to cook, clean and fit in a weekly manicure. Y girls were raised by working mothers who wanted and tried to live up to this ideal—but struggled with the reality. These girls saw their mothers as stressed and guilty, constantly juggling obligations and never feeling fully satisfied with every aspect of their lives. The example of their mothers has affected Y daughters in various ways. The majority want to continue their career through marriage and parenthood. Few young women anticipate being consistently dependent on the support of their partner.[31] In fact those who have seen their mothers struggle financially after divorce are intent on maintaining their own ability to earn a living. For example, Sasha's parents went through a rough time in their marriage when she was younger. She says 'I realised that my mother couldn't support herself financially and that terrified me.' For married Y girls like Renee, becoming a mother might alter their hours of work but not their commitment to its place in 'a balanced life'. Renee says:

> *I have worked hard to be where I am in my career. When we have kids, I want to return to work after twelve months. I have to go back; I just couldn't see myself sitting at home. I'd need that balance. If I had the option to go part-time, I would. Otherwise I'd be happy to return to full-time work.*

But whilst Y girls want to keep their careers ticking over, it won't be at the expense of their extracurricular obligations to family, friends and themselves. This desire for a stress- and guilt-free life has initiated a small but telling trend amongst Y women—the emergence of 'The New Wife'. The New Wife is well educated and ambitious. But, as Barbara Pocock found in her study of young people, work and care, having 'witnessed her mother's efforts to hold down a job while performing the bulk of child raising', The New Wife directs her smarts and ambition into 'finding a wealthy male bread-winner and raising their children'.[32] In her book *The New Wife*, Susan Shapiro Barash argues that Y women don't want what previous generations of women have fought so hard for—the right to work and have a successful career. In a newspaper article on the New Wife phenomenon, Shapiro Barash asserted that:

> *There is a whole bunch of really confident young women out there, who have a very good education but want a less stressful life. [They] can see how women in Generation X have left it too late to have children, or are being torn between the office and their babies. They intend to avoid the exhaustion, haggard looks and divorce by giving up full-time work.*[33]

However, these New Wives are in the minority. Their existence is not going to alter the character of work for this generation. For a Y-led reform of the workplace to occur, Y men have to come to the table, lobbying beside their partners for a more humane deal for working families. They have the potential to do this. They are a generation of young men raised by working mothers, who will marry and father children with working women. They have also been raised by often distant, workaholic fathers, who struggled with hands-on parenting.[34] Many Y boys don't want to be the fathers they grew up with. Whilst the early signs in terms of gender equity in the home aren't good, there is still hope that young men will, as Barbara Pocock says, 'lean against the door of workplace flexibility', fight for a fairer deal at work and contribute equally at home.[35]

If the life patterns of Generation Y pan out as predicted, it will be at least a decade or more before they commit to the kinds of obligations that keep people in work whether they like it or not—namely a mortgage and children. Until then, the bulk of Generation Y will constitute a volatile sector of the workforce, switching career paths, companies, taking off travelling, downshifting and moving home to take on further study. A job for life isn't an option. And even if it was, they aren't investing enough in work to want that. Why not? They want to avoid the harried lives of their parents. Instead, they want an interesting job that can fund a balanced life, one that involves a harmony of work, relationships, friends, fun, travel and life experience. As Jim puts it, Yers want to work to live rather than vice versa. At present, this generation presents a challenge to employers to be more flexible in their employment practices. If both Y men and women stick to their guns about achieving the right work/life balance, they may alter the world of work—for everyone.

CHAPTER 7

The world is a fucked-up place
»

IT WAS A RAINY WINTER'S day when I sat in a high school classroom draped in unrecognisable flags, waiting to interview a few of the 300 delegates to Oxfam's International Youth Parliament (IYP). This is an event that brings together youth leaders from around the world to workshop action plans for community-oriented projects in their countries of origin. My first interviewee was O'Neil Simpson, a tall and charming 24-year-old university student from rural Jamaica. He sauntered into the room, all smiles and kissed me on both cheeks like a long-lost uncle. O'Neil's home country is cursed with widespread poverty, alarming rates of HIV/AIDS infection and lawlessness which gives it one of the world's highest murder rates. When I met him, O'Neil was in the process of establishing a reading program in his rural community with the aim of not only improving literacy but stemming the growth of HIV/AIDS. He spoke clearly and passionately to me about health and education and about the sense of apathy and powerlessness amongst Jamaican youth. I asked him if he would ever consider a career in politics. He didn't think so. Political parties in Jamaica are an obstacle rather than an agent of change, he told me. His priorities were helping people to read and encouraging sexual responsibility. He talked about hope for a better future and the love he has for his home town, Mt Carey, near Montego Bay. He was inspired by the ways in which other conference delegates from places as diverse as Tonga and Zimbabwe have dealt with problems facing their communities.

Talking to O'Neil was an eerie experience. Here was a university student from rural Jamaica saying the same things about politics as someone like Hannah, a single mum living in western Sydney. Talking to other delegates, it became clear that while their activism is local, focused on the communities where they have the closest and most personal ties, they draw inspiration and energy from what is happening at the global level. They are connected to each other's struggles both in spirit and via the Internet (there was a frenzied swapping of hotmail accounts as I circulated amongst delegates at lunchtime). The problems of a young unionist in Indonesia can be interesting and relevant to the struggles of a health activist in the West Indies. What is left out, almost shunned, in this new 'local meets global' politics is the national and the party political. Political parties are the problem rather than the solution to the problems facing young people and their communities.

My encounter with O'Neil Simpson revealed some basic truths about Generation Y's attitude to politics. They are turned off, annoyed and distrustful of political parties, politicians and increasingly the media that is supposed to keep them honest. Few see mainstream politics as a legitimate way to exercise power or as a useful vehicle for changing the world. But despite being disengaged and disillusioned with conventional politics, they do care about political issues (or at least they feel guilty when they don't). Many are looking for alternative ways to get involved and so they focus on issues that affect them immediately and personally, at the local and the community level, or on international issues, something facilitated by information technologies without borders like the Internet.

In the minds of political scientists, Generation Y is just like the generation that preceded it—apathetic and anti-political. According to Gen X definers like Douglas Coupland, my generation has always seen party politics as 'corny—no longer relevant or meaningful or useful to modern societal issues, and in many cases dangerous'.[1] We were the slackers and the cynics. The term 'apathetic' was used to describe us with such regularity that it became the verbal equivalent of nails down a chalkboard. Of course, this charge of political apathy was forged out of an unfair comparison between the Boomers (those 1960s and 1970s radicals) and us. Unfair because there is ample evidence that young people have always felt left out and cynical when it comes to politics. In 1972, the year I was born, legendary *Rolling Stone* journalist Hunter S. Thompson covered the Nixon/McGovern presidential contest in his book *Fear and Loathing on the Campaign Trail '72*. For the young people he encountered on his trips around America 'politics was some kind of game played by old people, like bridge'.[2] These teenagers and 20-somethings—basically my parents' generation—were waiting around hoping that they would one day get a 'chance to vote for something, instead of always being faced with that old familiar choice between the lesser of two evils'. Thompson's observations challenge the notion that everyone back then had joined the revolution.

It is still common for journalists and political scientists to reiterate 'findings' that young people are 'not interested in and not very knowledgeable about politics'.[3] Howe and Strauss state that American Yers 'have never cared much about voting... or what goes on in Congress'.[4] Many studies in Australia have shown that there is a serious weakness in young people's understanding about how the political system works.[5] Fewer young Australians eligible to vote are enrolled (approximately 82 per cent in 2004) compared with older Australians (95 per cent).[6] There are significant blocks of young people who are dismissive of and even antagonistic to political acts like protest marches and petitions.[7] Yers generally admit to not understanding or caring much about traditional politics. For Trudi, a 24-year-old librarian, the world of politics 'just seems to go along' around her. She is more interested in her own world of dance classes, favourite TV shows and close friends.

If you were going to measure the political engagement of Generation Y according to statistics on youth membership of the major parties, then the charge of apathy would be justified. Party membership is comparatively low across all demographics of the population but it is particularly acute amongst young people. The membership of all Australian political parties is ageing. For example, a review in 2002 found that only around 7 per cent of ALP members were aged between 18–24.[8] The situation is the same in other democratic countries with the two-party system. In the United States, contributors to the two major parties are all much older than the typical voter.[9] In Canada, the average age of party members is 59 and only 6 per cent of party members are under 30 years of age.[10] And with an ageing population and a dropping birth rate, the average age of voters is going to keep rising. In 1971 the average age in Australia was 27 but today it is 36 and still headed up. As Y columnist Simon Castles observes, 'Politics is growing old with the population [and] it's only going to get greyer in the years ahead.'[11] Politics in the future will be less hip and more hip replacement.

Instead of seeing Generation Y's disinterest in party politics as evidence of their apathy, it should be seen as an indication of just how unappealing political parties have become. The reasons for Generation Y's distaste for the major parties is reflected perfectly in a Halloween episode of *The Simpsons*, entitled 'Citizen Kang'. In this episode Homer Simpson is abducted by aliens who take him to Washington where they replace political leaders Bill Clinton and Bob Dole just before an election. No one believes Homer when he tries to alert people to the fact that the two candidates are aliens in disguise planning to take over the world. In the end Homer manages to unmask the aliens in front of a crowd of voters, yelling 'America, take a good look at your beloved candidates—they're nothing but hideous space reptiles.' The aliens respond to their public unmasking calmly, telling the crowd: 'It's true, we are aliens. But what are you going to do about it? It's a two-party system; you have to vote for one of us.'

This is Generation Y's view of party politics. In their eyes, the two-party system doesn't provide any real choice. They feel that there isn't enough of a difference between the major parties to justify feeling strongly about one over the other. Whoever is running the country isn't really going to change your life so why bother? For Patrick, a 23-year-old law graduate, politics is 'uninspiring' because there are 'only slight differences' between the two major parties. For a generation that values choice and difference, similarity is a major turn-off. As far as Yers are concerned (and let's face it, they are not alone in this) politicians appear both alien and alike. Daniel says they come across as 'a club of conservative intellectuals rather than every day people', while 24-year-old Tara sees them as 'professionals who represent our parents' generation and their social values'.

Not only do political parties seem like alien territory, Generation Y feels that there is little that can be done to change them. Few think that you can really make a difference by joining a political party. For example, Blake sees party structures and discipline as forcing members 'to vote for something they believe is corrupt and unjust'. The major parties don't allow for enough internal democracy and freedom to satisfy the needs of a generation that expects flexibility and choice in all its endeavours. This is a generation that is enthusiastic about direct democracy. Its members get to choose who is the next Australian Idol or who gets evicted from the Big Brother house. The 'tow-the-party-line' mentality of the major political parties seems too simplistic, too constraining for a generation that is used to this kind of direct involvement in decision making.

If young people are, as Castles describes, 'the great unwashed of the electorate—ignored, rarely spoken about, and never, ever spoken to',[12] then it is no wonder they are disengaged from politics. However, 'apathy' just isn't an accurate way to describe the political attitudes of Generation Y. Whilst they might see politics as boring and unappealing, they aren't comfortable with their current levels of political ignorance. They believe they should know more about how the system works. For example, 83 per cent of those surveyed in the 2003 Democrats Youth Poll believed that students should be taught more about Australia's political and legal system at school. And Generation Y makes a vital distinction between caring about party politics and caring about the stuff of politics, the issues that matter. James, 23 years old and working in insurance, argues that while the 'care factor' is pretty low when it comes to who is in government, young people are concerned about how the country is run. Similarly, researchers have found that Yers have views and they have some idea about what is going on, but that concern hasn't translated into traditional forms of political behaviour like party membership.[13]

Rather than apathy, Y men and women project something more like powerlessness, either to change the political culture or to make progress with political issues. Tim, a unionist and father of one, believes that 'many young people think they cannot change anything so there is no point trying'. Even those who are more optimistic about the possibility of change set their sights pretty low. Laura knows that it's a cliché but she would 'like to make a bit of a difference'. Gone are the big, bold pronouncements of the Boomer era about changing the world and revolutionising society. When Yers do identify a possible change to society that can happen, it is usually something small but profound. Saving some trees in a public park. Raising money for a local community project. The achievement of filmmaker Morgan Spurlock, whose film *Super Size Me* put significant pressure on McDonalds to change its marketing techniques, is appealing to a generation that feels, as Barna says, that 'one person can make a difference in the world—but not much'.[14]

The media contributes to this sense that the world is constantly changing but is essentially unchangeable. Knowledge isn't always power—sometimes information overload can leave you feeling helpless. Young people feel inundated with a seemingly endless stream of bad news about the world, which increases their sense of powerlessness. For example, Mary Jane feels there is too much information and too many options. She says 'The world is a fucked-up place and it is very easy to feel overwhelmed and apathetic.' Media studies commentator Catharine Lumby believes that young people now have access to so much information about what's wrong with the world that they'd often prefer to watch a sitcom rather than sit through yet another news story about corruption, war, crime or disaster.[15]

In fact Generation Y is more likely to get its political information and views from a sitcom than from the morning newspaper. Media analyst Jason Sternberg found that since the 1990s young people have been reading, watching and listening to less current affairs than ever before.[16] They rarely watch the nightly news or read the paper. Those who do make an effort to follow the news media talk about it in the same way that older people talk about taking their vitamins. However, all this doesn't mean that the media isn't a major source of political information and a crucial shaper of Y's political outlook. Traditional media such as newspapers, television, radio and magazines are just a part of a number of information and communication technologies, now including cable television and the Internet, that influence the politics of Generation Y.[17] Howe and Strauss agree, arguing that young adults get their information about politics 'less through the usual adult news sources than through comedy shows, Internet web sites and chat rooms'.[18] Seen in this light, an article in *Marie Claire* will have a far greater impact on the political attitudes of Generation Y than the evening news. Yers also get their political education within the context of their personal relationships. Successive Democrats Youth Polls show that young people consider family, friends and teachers to be the most trustworthy sources of political information. Politicians are the least trustworthy.[19]

It's no great revelation to say that Generation Y is wary and cynical about politics. This is the natural result of growing up in a conspiracy-theory age where it is well accepted that governments and politicians cheat and manipulate in order to seize and hold onto power. Yers use words like 'lie', 'distrust' and 'corrupt' in connection with politics without any sense of false bravado. Academic Clive Hamilton believes that our culture breeds this attitude: 'Young people hear only the accusation that the political system is incurably corrupt—and they believe it.'[20] It seems that this is a generation that anticipates being duped by authority figures. For example, Laura isn't interested in politics because, she says, 'I feel like a lot of the stuff we are told isn't really the truth and I'm not someone who enjoys being lied to'. Martin, a 25-year-old musician, feels the same.

His interest in politics is curbed by the fact that he needs to know that he isn't 'being fed bullshit'. Why take an interest or invest in a system that you expect is going to lie to you about important stuff? Better to disengage than be fooled.

And the news media are no help in this regard. In young people's eyes, the media is part of the problem of politics, rather than an independent force informing people and keeping tabs on those in power. Daniel, an aspiring journalist himself, feels that politics is 'not about the issues but about scandals'. Patrick thinks that 'the culture of spin-doctoring and media management' in politics 'seems to preclude serious, informed public debate'. Tony, who openly describes himself as being 'clueless' about politics, questions whether in fact the media could provide him with reliable information even if he wanted to educate himself about current affairs. He says 'Even if I watched the TV or read the papers, I don't think I would be that much more informed because the news media have adapted to what people want to hear.' These sentiments are backed up by some interest-ing findings in the Democrats Youth Poll. In 1999, 29 per cent of poll respondents listed the media as the most trust-worthy source of political information. In 2003 that plummeted to 5 per cent, 1 per cent below the percentage point for politicians (who were at 6 per cent). According to Catharine Lumby, Generation Y has grown up in a time 'when distrust of journalists and media commentators is high'.[21] In her opinion, it is not surprising that politicians and jour-nalists are 'reviled for common reasons, since the two groups rely on similar research and tactics in their quest to win public approval'.[22]

If party politics is so unappealing and the news media so untrustworthy, what are the alternatives for Generation Y? As a response to the constraints and monotony of party politics, they have turned their energies towards local and community politics. This means that young people's activism has been largely invisible to political scientists. Young people are heavily involved in public life, but often in ways not conventionally recognised as 'political'. Ari Vromen, a leading Australian researcher on the civic behaviour of generations X and Y, argues that young people's political activism shouldn't be measured against some preconceived notion of what 'real' political behaviour is. Rather we need to look at the diverse ways in which young people participate in public life beyond party and electoral politics. Whilst they may not measure high on the scales of traditional political activity—donating money, contacting MPs, joining political parties or unions—the vast majority of them are involved in community, campaigning and protest activities.[23] Vromen found that young people were involved in church groups, parents' and citizens' groups, environmental and sporting organisations. (She also found that they are particularly willing to boycott products for political reasons). This mirrors trends in the United States, where youth volunteerism is at an all-time high. Journalist Drake Bennett argues that 'young America is awash in community service' and 'high school and college community-service activities have never been more extensive'.[24] Turning away from the national and the party political, Gen-Yers are taking a small target approach in their own political behaviour, focusing on organisations and issues that are closest to them. These seem easier to understand and easier to influence.

Yers combine this interest in local, community politics with an intense interest in international issues. This engagement with international politics started with Generation X and its anxieties about nuclear war and environmental disaster. Douglas Coupland's book is full of references to the biodegradability of objects and the certainty of a global environmental meltdown. This fear of environmental apocalypse hasn't diminished; it still provides a highly plausible premise for a major motion picture aimed at the Y market, having replaced natural disasters and nuclear war as the most likely threat to humanity. The political importance of the environment, coupled with celebrity-sponsored campaigns about everything from third-world debt to garment-worker exploitation, has ensured that today's young adults have a resolutely international focus when it comes to naming the political issues that matter to them. The state of our global environment is now part of a package of concerns for this generation that includes anti-corporatism, globalisation, international human rights, the rights of workers in third-world countries and peace issues. In fact, the anti-globalisation movement is dominated by young people, who have organised via the Internet massive protests focused on meetings of transnational organisations such as the World Trade Organization.[25] Naomi Klein describes this shift in her book *No Logo* as a shift from identity politics to global politics. She states that within the sphere of campus politics in particular there has been:

> *... a rather sudden change in political focus; five years earlier, [it] was all about issues of discrimination and identity—race, gender and sexuality. Now [students are] broadening out to include corporate power, labor rights, and a fairly developed analysis of the workings of the global economy.*[26]

This interest in the international over the national is driven by a number of factors. International politics certainly seems more glamorous. For 25-year-old consultant Sasha, national politics seems dull and trivial compared with international politics, which is more alluring and rich in the big issues. In the international arena, the stakes are higher and the divisions clearer. Generation Y, a well-travelled bunch, recognise this. Steve, who took off a year from his law studies to travel in South America, feels that 'in a lot of countries whoever wins an election could be the difference between life and death' whereas in Australia it means 'slightly different taxes'. Finally, and perhaps most importantly, technologies like the Internet have provided a virtual platform for a wide variety of political causes. These technologies have shaped young people's relationship with time and space. Quicker and closer connections create a wider political outlook. The plight of garment workers in Thailand doesn't seem like such a distant struggle if information about it can be obtained so quickly and easily via the Net. Online petitions, protest emails and donations can be dealt with in a matter of seconds.

So Yers favour international politics over domestic politics and as a consequence are more likely to support non-government organisations (NGOs) than political parties.

For example, in the eyes of Jenny and her friends, 'the major parties seem corrupt' and so they choose to be active in those NGOs that campaign on human rights, environmental protection and aid to foreign countries. Generation Y feels that joining Greenpeace or volunteering for Amnesty International is an easier and more worthwhile way to change things. Young people are more likely to volunteer or join organisations like Oxfam than they are major or even minor political parties.[27] Unlike political parties, NGOs seem more trustworthy, able and willing to make a difference.

Like NGOs, smaller political alternatives within the party system such as green parties are also attracting the support of young people.[28] Political scientist Anna Greenberg found that American trends in voting for third-party candidates confirm that 'Gen Y voters are more likely than any other generation to call themselves independents'.[29] The attraction of alternative political parties is a product of the general cynicism about mainstream politics and of doubts about whether the major parties present voters with any real choices or new ideas. Alternative political parties trade on their difference, emphasising that they provide a real alternative and clear policy positions within a system where all politicians look and sound the same. Green parties in particular also seem to be more democratic and offer supporters a real chance to participate. Yers believe that smaller parties as well as non-partisan organisations like NGOs are more honest and accountable. They haven't yet lost their souls.

Howe and Strauss argue that Generation Y has rejected the 'too cool to care' credo of Generation X and displays a genuine interest in volunteer work, community and local politics.[30] While some commentators persist in their description of Y as apathetic and politically clueless, in fact Yers are a principled and idealistic lot who are committed to making the world a better place.[31] They just don't see political parties or national politics generally as the way to create that better place. Generation Y expects to be deceived by politicians and manipulated by the news media. As a result, Yers have embraced the diversity, difference and challenge of international politics. They support NGOs and educate themselves via the new global soapbox of the Internet. They are active in local politics because it affects them more directly and because it seems possible to bring about some change there.

What might a future politics shaped by the values of Generation Y look like? A future Y politics will be a unique combination of Left and Right positions and perspectives. For Generation Y, the political distinctions between Left and Right are far less clear and relevant than they were for previous generations. These divisions once tightly structured national politics and public debate. They now mean little to a generation that has seen left-wing government embrace privatisation and deregulation and right-wing governments promote black women into positions of power. As a consequence of two decades of political change that have messed up the Left–Right political axis, Y's political worldview contains, what Anna Greenberg calls, 'a complicated mix of liberal and conservative perspectives'.[32] She argues that whilst young American voters have 'little interest in retirement security or reforming Medicare', they do think that 'government should do more to solve people's problems'.[33]

In general Yers are 'very individualistic about problem solving and supportive of market solutions' but they are also community and consensus oriented.[34] Attracting the Y vote means that political parties will have to rethink old orthodoxies and political commitments formerly designated as either Left or Right.

National politics will have to fully embrace both the local and the international to be relevant to Y voters. It will have to address everything from urban environments to deforestation in Asia—and draw connections between the two. For those who are politically engaged and radicalised, the politics of identity (focused around questions of race, sex, ethnicity and so on) will seem less important than the politics of anti-corporatism. Generation Y knows that money is power and in a world where the gap between rich and poor is growing every day, they see economic disadvantage as the greatest social handicap. Political parties need to recognise this and knit a political agenda that incorporates both the local and the international, and addresses the politics of economic disadvantage. In an institutional sense, Generation Y voters challenge political parties to either change or die. Parties themselves—their structures and their culture—must become more open, flexible and democratic if they are to recruit younger members. This is a generation that doesn't just value direct democracy and freedom of choice: it takes it for granted. Yers aren't going to pledge undying support for a political leader elected in an undemocratic way when their own culture gives them the power to choose the next Australian Idol. If political parties can't democratise or create a new 'local meets global' agenda that tackles problems relating to economic insecurity and disadvantage, then Generation Y will continue to turn away from national politics. Politicians will remain ageing aliens and political parties and processes will become part of a galaxy far, far away.

CHAPTER 8

It's painful to be sexy
»

NAOMI WOLF'S *The Beauty Myth* came out in 1990 when I had just finished high school. I had gotten over my adolescent obsessiveness with dieting and eating and was in the first flush of feminist zeal. The book really spoke to me, as it did to many of the other women I knew. Just as women were beginning to taste equality in the political sphere, the workplace and the bedroom, just as we were emerging as a well-educated, powerful and proud force in society, we were being thwarted by a cultural and media conspiracy that said we weren't good enough if we weren't thin. Thin, beautiful and young to be exact. All these political and social rights meant little if we were too weak from eating lettuce to claim them. This conspiracy—played out on the billboards, magazines and catwalks of the world—ensured that no matter how educated, powerful and proud we were, we would constantly feel less than adequate because we failed to live up to a near impossible standard of beauty set (largely) by an elite group of men.

The ideas in *The Beauty Myth* caught on and spread into popular consciousness. It put the issue of women and body image on the agenda of the very magazines it criticised.

It fed into government policies on women's representation in the media. And it made Naomi Wolf, with her flowing mane of hair and sparkly eyes, a Third-Wave superstar. She brought feminist ideas to a generation of young women, many of whom were reluctant to call themselves feminists.

The Beauty Myth provided me with a political answer to the silent questions I had as a teenager growing up with the pressure to look like Cindy Crawford. And my teens were the time when these pressures first emerged for Gen X girls. But for Generation Y, body obsession started in the tween rather than the teen years. Kristie is a 19-year-old economics student who attended an all-girls Catholic school. For her and her friends, anxieties around body image started 'quite early on', in the last few years of primary school. It was the same for Jenny who attended a co-ed public school. Girls at her school started to focus on their bodies 'really early, well before high school'. Jackie, who was educated in a regional area, blames this on the magazines like *Dolly* and *Girlfriend* which are targeted at primary school kids. She says 'There were more of these magazines around when we were growing up so concerns about body image started earlier than for older women.'

So when Y girls entered high school, the adolescent beauty pageant had well and truly commenced—and everyone was a contestant.[1] In her insightful and practical guide to what she calls 'Girl World', Rosalind Wiseman explains that by the time American girls hit 13 they are obsessed with their appearance and are constantly comparing themselves to each other. Beauty is vitally important to teen girls because it is the criterion that determines a high school's pecking order. Being pretty means being powerful. Again, awareness of this amongst Y girls began well before high school. At Jenny's primary school 'the two most unpopular kids were the smartest boy and the fattest girl'. Indeed, for fat girls, school is a special kind of hell. One of Trudi's high school friends was overweight and was mercilessly teased about it. Trudi says 'She hated school. I wouldn't be surprised if she tried to kill herself over it.' Being fat is such a blow to social status and acceptability that by the time Y girls entered high school, they were intimately familiar with the full arsenal of weight-loss techniques—dieting, extreme dieting, fasting, bingeing and purging, slimming tablets, diuretics, laxatives, cigarettes, coffee, energy drinks and food supplements. At Renee's all-girl Catholic school 'everyone was trying to lose weight'. A recent Australian study found that almost half of high school girls had issues about their weight and body image that were just as intense as those of girls being treated for eating disorders.[2]

Whilst eating disorders usually begin to emerge as a problem in the high school years, for many the obsession continues into young adulthood. Bulimia nervosa is growing steadily in young women. The Australian Longitudinal Women's Health Study showed that nearly 5 per cent of the 15 000 subjects in the 18–22-year-old age group were bulimic, and almost 20 per cent had symptoms of binge eating disorder.[3] Around 1 per cent of young Australian women are anorexic.[4] Whilst these eating diseases are a real public health concern, of greater social concern are the constant body-image stresses and food paranoias affecting the vast majority of young women. Health surveys have shown that a significant percentage of young women think they are heavier than they actually are.[5] On any given day of the year, 30 per cent of young Australian women are on a diet. Thirty one per cent of young women are underweight and about 40 per cent of those believe they should be thinner. Dieting has become expected behaviour for the women of Generation Y.

When Gen X girls were in our early teens, we wanted to look willowy like Molly Ringwald. In the early 1990s, when the supermodel phenomenon hit (ironically started by the video for George Michael's hit single 'Freedom'), it was about being tall and thin and having big boobs. But for Y women, the ideal body of today is even more unattainable than the 1980s slim model. It's not enough just to be skinny anymore. For example, as Jackie explains, women her age want to be 'more athletic-looking rather than just thin'. Sarah, a former ballet dancer, agrees. She says 'It isn't just the pressure to be thin, it is about looking healthy.' So now you need to be thin as well as healthy looking, which means muscular with toned abs. But you can't lose your feminine curves and big boobs are still a must. If you can manage a shapely bottom like J-Lo then that's a plus. This muscular, lean but feminine body type (apparently attained purely through yoga and the Atkins Diet) has been popularised by celebs like Geri Halliwell (in her post Spice Girls phase), Jennifer Aniston and Madonna. For the vast majority of young women, nothing short of good genes, cosmetic surgery and a tri-athlete's training schedule could produce such a body. Thin was easier.

Where is this intense and intensifying pressure coming from? It is more complex and pervasive than simply a conspiracy amongst men to keep women in check. But the fact is Y men are in general far less critical of women's bodies than women are. All the young men I spoke to, whilst recognising that attractiveness in women was related to their size and shape, wanted women to 'look healthy' and didn't find skinny women sexy. Like Antony, most Y guys are turned off by 'those underfed women with enormous heads' in fashion magazines. Y men have also absorbed the feminist line about women and body image and appreciate the relentless and unfair pressure on women to conform to a certain look. Brendan, a 22-year-old bank worker, believes that 'the body image adored by our society is created by a few very powerful people in the media' and is 'extremely damaging' to the women of his generation.

So if the pressure is not coming from men, where is it coming from? As it was for Xers, this obsession with looks is all about social survival and the desire to be part of the group. Y girls recognise that the close and competitive relationships amongst girls at school helped create and fuel early body-image paranoias. Once school is over and those relationships fade away or change, body obsession is less intense. If women have a supportive friendship group, they find it easier to cope with society's body fixation. But it can rear its ugly head again under certain circumstances. For example, Hannah, a young mum and student, feels that it is her social group and environment that determine her feelings about her body. Jenny, a public servant, recalls working in an office where the women spent so much time talking about weight that it started having an effect on her, making

her feel out of place. However, she says 'As soon as I got out of that environment, I felt much better.'

In these scenarios—schools, the workplace, social and friendship circles—the primary offenders are often women, not men. When it comes to body obsessiveness, women are their own worst enemy. Both X and Y women are painfully aware of even the slightest weight fluctuations not only in their own bodies but the bodies of friends, acquaintances, movies stars, you name it. Kerry, a 21-year-old Indigenous woman who works in local government, says 'I think that every woman is aware of her own body and also aware of the bodies of other women.' In her book *Anything She Can Do I Can Do Better*, Rachael Oakes-Ash calls this impulse to analyse other women's bodies 'The Compare and Despair Stare'.[6] In general, men are oblivious to the *corporeal minutiae* that consume the thoughts of their female peers. If a woman is healthy and attractive, with breasts and a pulse, then a Y guy counts himself as lucky.

As with everything Y, the media plays a crucial role in driving this fixation on the body. From the mid-1980s onwards, there was an explosion of public discussion about sexist and sexualised images of women in advertising and the media in general.[7] Whilst stories about the issue started to feature in women's magazines once *The Beauty Myth* was published, the beauty and fashion industries were generally reluctant to respond to public worries about women and body image. This was despite the increasing incidents of eating disorders in young girls and the connections drawn by health professions between these diseases and unrealistic media portrayals of women. As a result cosmetic companies like The

Body Shop have run advertising campaigns featuring older women and heavier women. Magazines like *Cosmopolitan* and *Cleo* now use 'real' models, ordinary girls of different shapes and sizes, as well as Size 14+ models in some of their fashion spreads. But these valiant attempts at downsizing society's body fascism are the exceptions rather than the rule. Y women are still assaulted on a daily basis by what Alissa Quart calls 'abvertisements' and an endless display of 'public flesh',[8] a barrage of perfect, exposed and often famous young bodies draped across the Internet, magazines, television, movies, clothing stores, in every conceivable corner of commercial and public space. Added to this is the fact that the majority of brand-name clothes advertised aren't made in larger sizes. Generation Y live in a branded world where the make of your clothes is a reflection of your personality and an indicator of cool. If branded clothes are only manufactured in smaller sizes then it makes it very difficult for a size 16 girl to be accepted into that branded world. The fashion media, man-ufacturers of branded clothes and their advertisers send the message to Y women (and men) that cool only comes in Size 12 and under.

Many young women, despite being seasoned and smart media consumers, believe that media representations of women have a profound effect on their own body image. Liselle, a 23-year-old student and mother of two, is hyper-aware that all the women's mags feature thin, tall women. She says 'Even when I read a book, I imagine the characters as being thin because that's all I see.' This brings us to an interesting paradox. Y women know that these images of perfect women are employed in advertising and magazines

to make them consume more. They know they are being manipulated via their own fears and insecurities. But awareness of this does not stop body obsession. In her work, Rosalind Wiseman found that 'Girls know that magazines, TV, and movies are in the business of making girls feel insecure so they'll buy their products . . . yet in spite of their awareness and sophistication, they still get sucked in.'[9]

A small percentage of Y women try to block out the images that fuel body obsession by steering clear of the media that contain them. For example, Sophie avoids magazines like *Cleo* because, she says, 'I feel like I have pretty low self-esteem as it is.' Claire used to buy women's magazines when she was a teenager and would 'wonder endlessly how a person could become so perfect'. She shuns them now because they 'depress' her. But for the majority of Y women, these images are everywhere, so powerful and seductive that it seems futile to resist them. For most women, even those with a detailed understanding of *The Beauty Myth*, body obsession is like a maximum security prison—a few might escape but most must learn to live in their cage and call it home. Whilst Simone, a student teacher and mother, thinks that too much emphasis is placed on body image, she also believes that 'when all your friends are gorgeous and thin and that's what the media focuses on, then it's hard not to be concerned'. Laura sums up the feelings of so many of her peers when she tells me:

I'd like the say it didn't matter to me but it does. It really does and I wish it didn't. Most days I'll say that as long as I'm healthy, I'm fine. Other days I'll say that as long

*as I fit into a size whatever, I'm fine. And then there are
the bad days...*

So the pressure to conform to a beauty ideal comes at young
women from all directions—from other women, society in
general and the media specifically. And like Rebecca, they
believe 'it is not going to change'.

What has changed since body image issues emerged
as a public concern in the 1980s is that young men are now
growing up burdened by their own 'beauty myth'. This goes
beyond the usual concerns about height, muscles and penis
size. There are now increasing pressures on young men to be
toned and cut. Until recently it was young women who were
consistently more dissatisfied with their bodies than young
men.[10] Now it seems that young men are becoming increasingly anxious about their bodies and their appearance.[11] In
this way, a certain state of equality has been reached, albeit
not the one Naomi Wolf was hoping for. Alissa Quart believes
that in their pursuit of a six-pack and hairless chest, 'the boys
of Generation Y are in solidarity with their long-suffering
female peers'.[12] But unlike women of their generation, Y
men are more self-conscious and less vocal about the growing
social pressures to look like the guys on the cover of *Men's
Health* magazine.

Yet again the difference between X and Y is noteworthy.
When I was at high school, all kinds of boys could be sexy
and popular with the girls—the beefed-up sports jocks, the
lanky artistic types, the smart guys in the debating team, the
stoned guys in the garage band. Generally it was the sporty
types that were at the top of the social pile. However, their

investment in being physically strong existed within the context of sporting success. They lifted weights, ran, cycled, whatever, in order to be better at football, rowing, tennis and so on. The scene has shifted for Y boys since they entered high school. The Y boy's body is no longer the vehicle for sporting performance, which used to be the end goal. Rather the perfect body *is* the goal, and you can take or leave sporting skills. The emphasis is on the appearance of strength rather than on strength itself. Peter West, one of Australia's foremost commentators on men's issues, argues that at the present time 'image is everything'. It's all about how the body appears rather than how the body functions.[13] For example, Lawrence tells me that amongst his friends there has been 'an explosion of interest in gyms and drinking those protein shakes'. However, his friends go to the gym seeking 'a kind of superficial benefit' rather than improved health. He says 'They pump iron to look big, not so they can play sport better.'

So Y guys are doing exercise to achieve that six-pack, not necessarily to improve fitness and sporting skill. They recognise they need to have muscles that people can *see*. This has led to an increased interest amongst Gen Y guys in going to the gym. Indeed, there is a thriving 'workout culture' amongst young men. I witness it every Thursday night as I do my 60 minutes of cardio at the local gym, where the women are out-numbered by young men. All kinds of young men in fact, different ethnic and social types, wandering around in pairs or in groups, lifting weights, spotting each other, counting silently to themselves as they strain (sometimes audibly) to lift dumbbells that I could barely shift with both hands. Many Y men workout alone as well as with friends on a regular basis. Daniel, a tall, lean university student, goes to the gym because he wants to 'develop his upper body'. He says, 'If it wasn't healthy, I don't know if I would stop. I want to look good. It's like gel in your hair or nice clothes. It's just something you do to make yourself more attractive to girls.'

This interest in pumping iron and looking buff is not a totally new phenomenon. Within body-building and gay culture, the gym-toned male body has always been a sought-after ideal. In thinking about the issue of gay men and body image, we enter a realm of body consciousness that makes what women go through seem tame. For straight men there might be some pressure but many can opt to ignore most of it. For gay men, there is no option. Scott, a 25-year-old student, believes gay men are 'obsessed with every aspect of the body from penis size to chest size'. He says 'There is always something new—my thighs are too big or not muscly enough.' Martin agrees, saying that young gay men must constantly look good and be 'impeccably dressed'. Whilst shows like *Queer Eye for the Straight Guy* have assisted with gay visibility and tolerance, they have also added to the pressure to always 'be fantastic'. It also seems that gay men are more likely to undergo cosmetic surgery procedures than their straight counterparts. Scott knows lots of gay men who indulge in 'low level body modification' like collagen injections. Like women, gay men are used to fake tanning, body waxing, laser, skin peels and various forms of beauty pain to conform to the physical type idealised in their culture. Because gay men have been obsessed with their body image for longer than their straight counterparts, straight men now have to carefully negotiate that line between looking like a metrosexual and looking gay.

But since the late 1980s—the time of Calvin Klein ads on giant billboards, Arnold Schwarzenegger and Jean-Claude van Damme films—that ideal has extended to become the goal of men outside those sub-cultures. What is a relatively new phenomenon is the interest amongst Y men with dieting and a concern about becoming fat, something that was previously the exclusive terrain of women. Again this concern with dieting and fatness starts at a young age. Dr Murray Drummond, an expert on male eating disorders, has found that since the 1990s young men, even those in their early teens, have started exercising and avoiding unhealthy foods in order to stay slim and began expressing serious concerns about getting fat.[14] Young men are responding to a general pressure on men to look leaner and more toned. On any given day it is estimated that at least 17 per cent of men are on some sort of diet.[15] Up to 10 per cent of diagnosed anorexics are male.[16] Both Y men and women have noticed this increased interest amongst Y men with dieting and being overweight. Christopher, for example, who doesn't go on diets himself, knows lots of guys who try fad diets 'in the quest for the perfect body'. Renee's younger brother is 'very athletic, toned and has lost a lot of weight'. She says 'He is very health conscious and into looking a certain way.' Claire's 22-year-old brother is just as conscious of his body as any woman is. 'At one time, we thought he might be anorexic because he was thin and always talking about his weight and asking if he looked good enough,' Claire says.

As is the case with young women, young men's growing obsession with a perfect body (what Alissa Quart calls 'abdomen-mania')[17] is related to media representations: men's magazines like *Men's Health*, advertisements for bed sheets, underwear, jeans, aftershave or simply the cinematic vision of a half-naked Brad Pitt in *Troy*. Twenty-one-year-old Daniel says that media images of 'all these built-up Adonis types walking around without shirts' take their toll on him after a while, encouraging him to workout more so that he doesn't feel 'inadequate'. Again, media images of perfectly formed male bodies have been linked not only with the rise of anorexia amongst young men but also with reverse anorexia or 'bigorexia', the excessive concern about being big or muscular.[18] Sports scientist Paul Haslem describes an increasing obsessiveness amongst young men with looking big. For these Y men, training and diet literally take over their whole lifestyles in their attempt to achieve a muscular look.[19]

Interestingly, Y guys (the straight ones at least) believe the pressure to look muscular and trim comes from girls as much as from the media. A man is taking his life in his hands if he suggests that his girlfriend should maybe shed a few pounds. (Every guy knows the obligatory response to 'does my bum look big in this?') But women are getting more assertive about what they like about men's bodies and don't have much trouble telling guys to lose the gut and cut back on the beer and hamburgers. Whilst he might be confused about what women want emotionally, a Y man knows what they are attracted to physically. Steve, a law student and club cricketer, feels that 'there is this pressure to look athletic and strong' because girls want 'a healthy, muscular looking body'. Daniel agrees. He says 'You'll hear girls talking about how this guy with his shirt off in a Calvin Klein ad is so hot. Of course we take that in and we want to look like them.'[20]

Many young men recognise that societal pressures on their bodies don't really compare to the long-standing and relentless pressures on women. Jim, a post-graduate student, knows that despite all the 'rippling ab pretty boys' that populate our culture, 'the use of women's bodies over men's to sell commodities to men *and* women remains overwhelming'. Tim agrees that in terms of body image 'there is incredible pressure on everyone these days, but it is mostly targeted at women'. Y girls are less sympathetic about the plight of men, perhaps for good reason. Madelaine argues that 'compared to the stuff women have put up with for years' the pressure on men to look good is 'irrelevant'.

The final and, in many ways, most important development in our society's obsession with youth and beauty is the rise and rise of cosmetic surgery. In *The Beauty Myth*, Naomi Wolf dedicates a chapter to cosmetic surgery. If that book was written today the issue would no doubt consume much more page space. Gen-Yers were born during the 1980s, which was the 'Dawn of the Surgical Age'.[21] By the end of that decade, cosmetic surgery was the fastest growing 'medical' speciality in the United States. By 1988 more than two million Americans, at least 87 per cent of them female, had undergone a procedure.[22] But, as Brigid Delaney points out, even Wolf at her most alarmist and cynical couldn't have predicted that it would soon become acceptable for teenagers to resort to cosmetic surgery.[23] But that is fast becoming the case. In the United States teenagers account for 4 per cent of the cosmetic surgery market.[24] The Australian Society of Plastic Surgeons doesn't keep statistics; however, in a television current affairs program its president Alf Lewis told of a growing trend in youth cosmetic surgery.[25] Even the very young and beautiful—fashion models—are taking the surgical route in order to be perfect and thus more competitive in their chosen profession. Not only are more young models having cosmetic surgery, they are also having surgery earlier, as young as 19 or 20, when they haven't even started to age.[26]

It comes as no surprise then that many a Y girl has spent her teenage years discussing the issue of cosmetic surgery, fantasising with her friends in the school yard about what procedures she would get done when she was older. In 2000 the US magazine *Seventeen* found that 25 per cent of its teen readership had considered liposuction, tummy tucks or breast augmentation, while 12 per cent had considered nose jobs.[27] In 2001 there was a much publicised case of a British mother giving her daughter a breast enlargement for her 16th birthday.[28] Many of the Y women I spoke to nominated at least one procedure they wanted done when they were younger. Laura wanted liposuction on her butt. Arya wanted her tummy tucked. Louisa wanted a nose job. Lee-Ann and many, many others wanted breast implants. Unlike their Gen X older sisters, Y girls spend their younger years believing cosmetic surgery could solve their body image woes.

This adolescent fantasising took place within a cultural and media environment in which coverage of cosmetic surgery was beginning to escalate. Y girls grew up reading stories about celebrity surgery successes and disasters. Now cosmetic surgery is a consistent topic in gossip magazines like *Who* and *People* and the basis for reality shows like *Extreme Makeover* and TV dramas like *Nip/Tuck*. Alissa Quart states that the young women who now seek surgery 'can't imagine a time when there wasn't so much media coverage and salesmanship of these bodily correctives'.[29] All this publicity has had a mixed effect. The horror stories might dissuade some girls from turning their boob job fantasy into a reality. But other Y girls have become immune to the shock of seeing bloody scars and scalpel marks, putting it down to the price you pay for the perfect body.

For Gen Y girls, cosmetic surgery isn't just confined to the sphere of fantasy, the subject of teenage dreams and media gossip. They see cosmetic surgery around them in daily life. Many Y girls have friends who have had boob jobs, nose jobs, lips injected with silicon, ears pinned back and so on. Maybe a Y woman's mum or aunt has had a face or breast lift. As former ballet dancer, Jackie, says plastic surgery is everywhere and 'You go to the gym and you see boob jobs every day.' In my interviews I only found a small number of Gen Y girls who were opposed to cosmetic surgery on ethical grounds. For most, the only real barriers are the money and the pain. Some worry about the invasiveness of full-on surgery but feel much more comfortable with supposedly non-invasive procedures like Botox. Many Y girls consider Botox the safer option; a few needle pricks during your lunch break and you look five years younger. In a newspaper article on young people and cosmetic surgery, Alf Lewis predicts that even if Y women don't see surgery as an option now 'by the time they turn 30, collagen implants or a shot of Botox may seem as natural as booking an appointment for a haircut and colour'.[30]

This all means that cosmetic surgery has become 'naturalised',[31] simply one more option in an endless list of possible body beautification techniques. Women of all ages are used to body modification of some sort. Waxing, laser, manicures and pedicures, wonder bras, high heels, underpants that hold your tummy in and so on all change the look of your body and involve varying levels of discomfort and pain. It seems that girls are starting with these kinds of beauty rituals at a young age. Once they reach their late teens and early 20s some young women have not yet learnt to accept their God-given physical characteristics and are looking for something extra. Many Gen Y girls view all body modification procedures as existing along a continuum, from make-up and shaving to skin peels and Botox to boob jobs and face lifts. Where you draw the line becomes a question of personal choice and circumstance. Even Y guys agree. Kristie's partner James isn't bothered by the idea of cosmetic surgery. He says 'It is no different than putting on anti-wrinkle cream. It is all artificial modification.'

Cosmetic surgery now hovers on the border of fantasy and reality within Generation Y culture. Is it a genuine option or something only rich women and movie stars do? In this regard, the connections between celebrity and cosmetic surgery are particularly relevant and powerful. We live in an age of celebrity flesh flashing, where women like 20-year-old Kerry yearn to 'have a figure like a Hollywood star'.[32] Today's young women are surrounded by more exposed and famous flesh than girls of previous generations. Stars like Britney Spears and Halle Berry are displayed semi-naked on album covers, movie posters, in music videos, on the covers of boys' and girls' mags and on the red carpet, as Alissa Quart writes, 'revealing all their natural or newly acquired charms'.[33] Quart believes that with cosmetic surgery, Y girls 'can buy and then become the perfect profiles of the media stars and movie heroines' they admire. Young girls request a nose like Nicole Kidman or lips like Angelina Jolie. Surgeons reported an increasing interest in breast implant surgery amongst young girls after Britney Spears's rumoured augmentation.[34]

Britney denies those rumours of a boob job, but other celebrities haven't been so coy. Whereas cosmetic surgery was a closely guarded secret in Hollywood's bygone era, many celebrities have talked openly about it including Pamela Anderson, Melanie Griffith, Courtney Love and supermodel Iman. Other famous women like Dannii Minogue, Nicole Kidman, Sharon Stone, Demi Moore and Meg Ryan have clearly 'had work done' and are thus able to remain well-paid Hollywood actresses. Celebrities' embrace of the surgeon's knife in an effort to stay beautiful and employable has had a number of effects. First, it firms up the associations between surgery, glamour and success. Second, it makes cosmetic surgery seem less risky. As Quart comments, plastic surgery is 'possible and commonplace enough among the celebrity class not to seem dangerous for an ordinary person'.[35] Catharine Lumby argues that celebrities 'have become central figures in the social imagination, the ones which symbolise wider shifts in the way we conceive ourselves'.[36] This goes beyond young girls idolising movie stars and trying to emulate their fashion sense. Rather, all the images and dialogue associated with celebrity bodies create a broad and powerful context within which women, especially young women, negotiate their own body-image issues.

That being said, few Y women actually say they want to get cosmetic surgery so they can look like Cameron Diaz. Instead most co-opt the broad rhetoric of feminism to justify a desire for surgical alteration. Wanting cosmetic surgery is not about conforming to outside pressures to look thin and perfect. Nor is it about pleasing your man, who wants you to look like the girls on the cover of *Maxim* or *FHM*. Rather, it is about your own personal needs, self-empowerment, happiness and freedom. Wolf recognises this in *The Beauty Myth* when she writes that 'Women are not cutting their breasts open for individual men ... in a diseased environment, they are doing this "for themselves".'[37] Many Gen-Yers, both male and female, seem to think that if you aren't comfortable with yourself and you want to make a change, then cosmetic surgery is okay. If it makes you happier, then why not? Even the more analytical Y souls like Claire are undecided about whether cosmetic surgery is justified. She has yet to work out whether it is 'a form of subservience to an external influence or a right of an individual to control what they do to their own body'. Others see cosmetic surgery as a possible requirement for women's employment and promotion. Surgical brochures emphasise career pressures on women to look youthful.[38] A private hospital website in Australia states that one of the reasons people might get cosmetic surgery is economic. It states 'They see that they will be more likely to get jobs if they appear younger.'[39] Cosmetic surgery becomes an option in light of this generation's need to feel confident and happy in the face of an uncertain and unfair world. If it gives you the edge in the workplace or boosts your self-esteem in the dating game, then go for it.

For Y men, cosmetic surgery isn't a consideration; none of the young men I interviewed saw it as an option. Although, Curtis, in his own candid fashion, says he would consider cosmetic surgery if he became aware that his appearance was severely restricting his job, social or relationship prospects. However, that being said, sports scientist Paul Haslem knows of young gym junkies who have implants in their shoulders, pecs and calves to achieve a desired look.[40] A website for a cosmetic surgery clinic sells the benefits to men in the following terms:

> More men in our society are requesting cosmetic surgery to look young and fit. From having a trimmer waistline, rejuvenated face, more hair on the head to a better-shaped nose, cosmetic muscle enhancement, implants and sculpting techniques to improve muscle contours of otherwise healthy men such as pectoral muscle implants and calf implants.[41]

This increasing willingness by men to go under the knife is another example of the odd state of gender equality we have reached in the arena of body image.[42]

There is something deeper in the cosmetic surgery phenomenon than a simple human desire to look good. We live in a make-over culture, where people believe if they look different, their lives will be different. The idea that looking different can change your life is the basis of reality TV, feel-good episodes of *Oprah* as well as teen films such as *She's All That*, *The Princess Diaries* and *Miss Congeniality*. Alissa Quart argues that the 'instant transformations' promised in these TV shows and films is 'very much a Generation Y phenomenon, an obvious way to speak to kids who have been taught to believe that respect and a new self are merely a new slip dress or a new lip gloss away'.[43] But when a new hair colour and clothes don't suffice then technology steps in to provide an 'instant' fix such as a smaller nose or bigger breasts.

This belief that we can make ourselves over— 'psychiatry with a knife' as it is known—is connected to that potent neo-liberal idea that so many Gen-Yers have absorbed in a largely uncritical manner. You can be whoever you want to be. There are unlimited options and no limits to your personal freedom and right to choose. As Wolf observes, the desire for personal reinvention via cosmetic surgery is 'the American dream come true'. She writes 'One can re-create oneself "better" in a brave new world', a world which requires you to be braver and braver as time goes on.[44] As Generation Y gets older, cosmetic surgery may not just be an option; it could become an imperative. Academic Meredith Jones argues that Yers may well be accused of 'letting themselves go' or 'failing to achieve their full potential' if they allow their bodies to age naturally. Jones believes that in the future, signs of age or any slight physical defect may well be characterised in the same way that obesity is characterised now, as indicating a lack of ambition, self-confidence or self-discipline.[45] In the light of this, beauty technologies will not be viewed as repressive, but rather something that smart girls (and guys) use to 'fast-track themselves to economic security, independence and personal power'.[46]

Y men and women have absorbed *The Beauty Myth* critique and are fully aware of how the media tries to capitalise on their insecurities to sell more ad space for the manufacturers of beauty products and diet pills. They are concerned about the extent to which our society emphasises appearance over substance. Despite all this, body obsessiveness is alive and well in Generation Y and shows no sign of abating. We are now at the state of a new kind of equality, where Y men join Y women in a mutually reinforcing quest to look like the headless models on a late-night infomercial for The Ab Blaster. The public debates around body image that started in the 1990s haven't managed to curb society's obsession with the female body beautiful. Instead, this obsession has simply expanded to include the male body beautiful. Alissa Quart observes that, 'Once there was a hope among feminists that girls could be taught to escape their oppressive body project. This has not occurred. Now, boys partake in it as well.'[47]

Yers know all this focus on the body is superficial and unfair. But they also know that we live in a world where, according to Catharine Lumby, 'beauty matters more than truth'.[48] There is a huge price to pay—socially, sexually and even financially—if you ignore societal pressures to be thin, young and beautiful. In a precarious world, you want to fit in, to succeed, and to remain confident in a climate that seeks to undermine that confidence at every turn. In the face of

Y all this, an Atkins regime and nose job seems like a small price to pay for social acceptance, sexual confidence and career success. It might be painful to be sexy, but not being sexy can hurt much more.

CHAPTER 9

We decide what's cool
»

WHEN I WAS 14 YEARS old, I went on a family holiday to Thailand. It was my first experience of Asia. I remember the trip vividly, especially the open-air markets full of bootleg videos and tapes. Accompanied by my mother, I spent days wandering down rows and rows of makeshift shops that were flogging fake everything—Gucci bags, Chanel sunglasses and Benetton luggage. I recall one stall selling fake Lacoste polo shirts, a status item within my friendship group at the time. This stall was also selling the little alligators that appear on the chest of each shirt. They were lying all jumbled up in a cardboard box, like some grossly inhumane zoo. My mother suggested, 'Why don't you buy some? Then all your clothes can be Lacoste.' Like any self-respecting teenager, I dismissed her suggestion as crazy. 'But no one will know that it's a fake,' she urged me. Yes, but I would. I knew that a fake could never radiate the warmth of the genuine, branded item. My teenage heart would not be soothed by a Thai rip-off, no matter how close it was to the real thing. I wouldn't be seen dead in one of those shirts now. I've moved on to other brands more acceptable within my social circle. Neverthe-less the power of the logo still works its magic on me and every kid who grew up wanting them and what they represent. Generation X spent its teen years schooled in the allure of the brand. Generation Y took it in as pre-schoolers.

Generation Y is the first genuine consumer generation, a group who started spending and dictating the spending habits of others at an early age. The Y childhood years saw a rising public concern for the safety of children and a new and intense focus on children's welfare and happiness. As a consequence, Y children spent less time outside involved in unsupervised play and more time inside, semi-supervised by the television whilst stressed parents juggled with the demands of work and home. Manufacturers and their advertisers saw the opportunities opened up by this adult interest in children's wants and desires and the role of TV as babysitter. Through TV they had a captive audience of kiddy consumers whose time-pressured parents were guilty enough and wealthy enough to start giving into their offsprings' newly created demands for the latest toy, video game and snack food.[1] In their study of parental work, guilt and consumption, researchers Barbara Pocock and Jane Clarke looked at how changing patterns of parenting have driven new levels of spending.[2] They found that Boomer parents who worked long hours attempted to make up for their absence by buying more stuff for their Y kids. This 'substitution of stuff for time' or 'contrition through spending' was an early influence on Y attitudes to consumption. Emotions such as love, friendship and forgiveness became linked to consumer behaviours such as shopping and gift giving.

As children, Yers were the prime movers of current, emerging and future consumption trends. These kids were seen to represent three different markets. First the 'pocket money' or 'weekend job' market, consisting of the direct money Yers spent on things like entertainment, food and clothing. However, this accounted for little when compared to what Howe and Strauss call the 'kidfluence' or 'the backseat consumer' market.[3] Unlike their X older siblings, Yers had their say over the consumer choices of the entire household, from grocery purchases to electrical goods, cars, holidays and houses. Growing up, Y kids influenced more than 70 per cent of their parents' clothing and food purchases.[4] Finally, Y children represented a lucrative long-term and future market. Advertisers believed that if brand loyalty could be secured when the consumer was young and vulnerable, it would be carried through to adulthood.[5] Give them the child until she is seven and they will give you the consumer.

Since childhood, the power of the Y dollar has grown and grown. In fact, one of this generation's defining characteristics to date has been its buying power.[6] Generation Y has been described by Howe and Strauss as 'a consumer behemoth, riding atop a new youth economy of astounding scale and extravagance'.[7] This has created an explosion of market research companies focused, sometimes exclusively, on finding out what teens and young adults think, want and feel. There isn't a company or corporation, big or small, that doesn't want to know what this group values and desires. If they can understand the Y market and communicate effectively with Y consumers, then corporations practically have a licence to print money. Yers are enthusiastic and indefatigable consumers. They learned to shop early and often. Shopping malls, with their heavily branded and familiar architecture, are the places they work and socialise.[8] Shopping is not a domestic chore for them; it is a hobby, a sport, even a way of life. Their income is mostly disposable. They are spenders rather than savers.[9] They are comfortable with levels of credit card debt that would make their elders blanch.[10] They have lived in a time of unprecedented economic prosperity, where products that were formerly considered luxury items, like designer clothes and electronic goods, are now lifestyle necessities.

Generation Yers' reasons for consuming are no mystery. They are not unlike the reasons for Xers' or Boomers' consumerism—instant gratification, desire for material possessions, an expression of identity, emotional release or simply the need to replace a worn-out pair of shoes. However, for Generation Y, consumption operates within a different economic context than Boomer consumption, with problematic consequences for their long-term prospects. Because of their age and the rising price of housing, Yers have few assets on which to earn capital gains. Despite this, they spend at the speed of their elders, who hold the bulk of the assets in our society including housing. The result has been a big structural shift in wealth. In his report on the financial status of the different generations, Chris Richardson found that X and Y hold just 22 per cent of the nation's wealth with the remaining 78 per cent 'comfortably tucked into the pockets of those born before 1961'.[11] This is a generation that keeps on spending but doesn't have the wealth (either at the moment or in the near future) to support the habit.

Despite all this, Generation Y shows no signs of slowing down its consumption habits. The drive to spend is partially fuelled by the fact that for many of them, especially those urban dwellers, the great Australian dream of owning a house and starting a family is a distant, almost unreachable, goal. Saving seems impossible. A mortgage means a harsh depression of lifestyle. Moving to a more affordable area means moving away from all-important friendship networks. And so Generation Y's income goes towards small investments such as clothes, electrical goods, travel, music, entertainment, some of which need updating or replacing every few years. Again this disadvantages Yers in the long term. As Carrie in *Sex and the City* discovered, by the time you reach your mid-30s, you might have a killer wardrobe with a stack of Manolo Blahniks but you will still be renting your one-bedroom apartment. Coupland sketches this scenario with pinpoint accuracy in *Generation X*—Andy, the main character, is an Xer; his brother Tyler is a Generation Y 'Global Teen prince'. Tyler and his friends have:

> ... *wardrobes full of the finest labels ... and they can afford them because like most Global Teen princes and princesses, they all live at home, unable to afford what few ludicrously overpriced apartments exist in the city. So their money all goes on their backs.*[12]

This observation is less a criticism than it seems. Without the huge sums of money required to buy property or the security of a 'job for life', spending on things like 'travel, clothes and technologies seems like a good alternative for both X and Y.[13] However, this desire to have things *now*, regardless of the long-term consequences, is also the result of a certain attitude, the 'go on, you deserve it' approach to spending that advertisers exploit so cleverly. The question 'I might deserve it but can I afford it?' often doesn't get asked by consumers, especially Y ones.

You can't talk about the rise of Generation Y as a target market and a consumer force without considering the rise of the logo. According to Alissa Quart, author of *Branded*, Yers have 'grown up in the age of the brand', in a 'contemporary luxury economy' where brands like Nike, McDonalds, Disney, Levi's and so on were as familiar to them as the names of their own friends and relatives.[14] Now that Yers are young adults, brand identification is still at an all-time high and shows no sign of dropping.[15] These young adults can't remember a time when logos and brand names weren't tattooed onto every conceivable product, splayed across every public and private surface, popping up when you log into your email, turning the bodies of sports celebrities, movie stars and practically everyone else into walking advertisements. Quart believes that films popular amongst Generation Y like *Legally Blonde* 'celebrate brands in their dialogue' to such an extent that they become like supporting actors.[16] Logos and brand names are now so omnipresent, they form the wallpaper of daily life.

Branded culture is a powerful driver of consumerism amongst Generation Y. Quart writes that teens and young adults now 'need' luxury products—that new lipstick, sports shoe, DVD or handbag—rather than simply want them.[17] And in so many ways branded culture is the force that determines what is a necessity rather than a luxury. Lawrence, a 22-year-old law student and part-time IT worker, doesn't consider himself to be particularly brand conscious. Nevertheless he wants an iPod. 'I just need one' he told me, in the way a pregnant woman says 'I need a toilet', with a palpable sense of desperation.

At the same time as the distinctions between luxury and necessity break down, the associations between brand names, celebrity and glamour within Y culture are reinforced. In *No Logo*, Naomi Klein argues that in the branded world, celebrities can become brands and at the same time brands can become stars in their own right.[18] Magazines like *Cleo* and *Cosmopolitan* have movie, music and TV stars on their covers and inside tell you exactly what products will give you Sarah Jessica Parker's sexy evening look. In this way, consumerism and celebrity worship are intertwined. If Meg, a fashionable arts student, sees a particular brand-name dress or lipstick on her favourite actress, then naturally she wants to buy it. In this way, a famous face reinforces the aura of the product. The celebrity associated with both the face and the product is enhanced. Girl-culture critic Susan Hopkins states that marketers 'aim to build a relationship between girls and their celebrity heroes, a relationship which might then be channelled towards increased consumption'.[19]

The links between identity, desire and consumption have been well-analysed by writers like Alissa Quart and Naomi Klein. These authors have illustrated the complex ways in which brands define those who consume them. I shop therefore I am. Very simply, when a Y consumer fronts up with his Billabong shirt at the cash register, he is unconsciously asking himself two questions: 'Who am I? Who do I want to be?'[20] For someone like Maddy, wearing clothing from Esprit or Sportsgirl is all about aspiring to be something more than just a single mum living with her parents. Maddy says 'When you go out in brand-name clothes, it makes you feel good. You are not just a single mother—you are a single girl as well.' This attitude to brand names demonstrates Catharine Lumby's belief that 'We don't just buy stuff—we buy the idea of stuff.'[21] Clive Hamilton argues that 'We all live with high levels of denial about the connection between our buying habits and the social statements they make.'[22] Not so for Generation Y. They have little trouble acknowledging that what they buy says something about who they are and who they want to be.

Despite their recognition of the strong connections between consumption and identity, Gen-Yers challenge the idea that they are wholly captive to branded culture. Many of them are irritated by commentary that characterises them as easily sucked in by advertising. Critics of commercialisation disagree. All they see is an army of consumer youth-zombies, manipulated by corporations and their media into buying lots of stuff they don't need. So there is a tug of war at the centre of public discussions about branded culture and Y consumers. Are they slaves to the logo, or creative and media-savvy consumers kicking arse in the marketplace? Are they players or are they pawns?

The reality is that Y consumers are both—both players and pawns in a cultural, social and economic environment where the connections between identity, desire and friendship are much more complex than older generations believe them to be. Yers are undeniably brand conscious. They are conformist in their consumption habits. They are influenced (although often unconsciously) by a desire to fit into the tastes and trends of their friendship group. With some purchasing choices, they gravitate towards the brands of their childhood. But they are also notoriously fickle and difficult to market to. They practice low-level forms of brand resistance and worry about the effects of rampant consumerism on our society. Yet they still believe that a branded item is better quality and more reliable than its no-name equivalent.

One of the emerging truisms about Generation Y is that Yers are conscious of brands but not loyal to them. They are known for having short attention spans and don't give a second thought to abandoning one brand name for another. Australian market researcher, David Chalke, describes Y as a 'promiscuous bunch' of consumers who 'lack brand loyalty and are prepared to try anything new'.[23] American research has found that Yers are 'more likely than other consumers to buy a product on the spur of the moment and change brands if the mood strikes'. Only one in five young Americans shop for a particular brand, compared with one in three fellow consumers who shop for specific brands at age 60.[24] It is clear that whilst Yers like 19-year-old Laura admit to being brand conscious, they are loath to describe themselves as brand loyal. She says 'I don't like people who stick to the same things or are too loyal to a brand.'

What is at the root of this lack of loyalty? Social researchers like Hugh Mackay believe that brand disloyalty is part and parcel of this generation's 'pragmatic and faddish' attitude to everything (except, of course, to friendship).[25] According to Mackay 'If they're not expecting to stick to one partner, one job, or one course of study, why would they expect to stick to one brand?'[26] As an extension of this, their disloyalty to branded commodities is a form of disloyalty to the corporations that produce them. Generation Y sees big corporations as untrustworthy and undependable. Why would you invest your loyalty in a big corporate organisation when it won't return the favour?

Y's generally fickle consumer persona is also tied to its belief in its own power as consumer. Yers truly believe that they decide what succeeds in the marketplace. They dismiss arguments that it is corporations and advertisers that control their habits and tastes. Rather, they are the ones who decide what is popular and cool (and this is always changing, just to keep everyone on their toes).[27] This confidence of Yers in their own consumer autonomy is connected to their confidence as media consumers. Growing up, Yers were used to being treated like a 'target market'. Before they could read and write, they were the focus of high-velocity marketing techniques and advertising.[28] This upbringing has produced a youth market that is extremely media-savvy and derisive of those marketers who insult their intelligence with gimmicks and cheap tricks.[29] Yers exhibit great disdain for advertising that uses patronising images and language and that tries to sell them 'cool' in obvious ways. They are cynical and untrusting of advertising and marketing promises. Daniel, for example, sums up the view of his Y peers in the following terms:

> *It is trendy to argue that young people consume via brand names and just consume what's cool. It must always be remembered that we don't get told what's cool. We decide*

what's cool. We make our own choices. We are not dopes.
We don't just buy something because we are told to
buy it.

Like Daniel, a healthy percentage of Generation Y expresses and practises low forms of resistance to branded culture. The average 19-year-old believes that whilst brands were important in high school, they aren't really important anymore. Now they only buy stuff they like, stuff that's good quality. They aren't going to be fooled by advertising into buying something just because it has a logo stitched on it. Lawrence is less into brands now than when he was a teenager. He says 'I very rarely dress in brands now. I find them ugly and tacky.' Yers reject obvious forms of brand chasing. Martin doesn't like 'big labels on the outside of things' (although he loves his Versace jeans). In addition to this aversion to crass forms of logo display, Yers believe that our society's obsession with consumption and material possessions is ultimately destructive. Patrick is 'very cynical about our empty consumer culture'. He says 'The amount of cash wasted on the vain and the superficial in our society concerns me deeply.' In their work, researchers Pocock and Clarke found that 'young people share a well-developed critique of materialism'.[30]

But these low level and subtle forms of brand resistance and concerns about materialism exist in tension with a general, and usually stronger, desire for branded items. And there is plenty of evidence that in relation to particular acts of consumption, Yers have carried through childhood loyalties into adulthood. The brands they grew up with as children evoke feelings of comfort and familiarity, like chicken soup for the consumer soul. For example, when shopping in the supermarket, Jackie doesn't check prices or go for the cheapest option. Instead, she opts for the brands she grew up with because they seem more reliable. Whilst Kerry doesn't care much about brands when it comes to clothing or shoes, she still prefers food and grocery items from 'the good old brands' that remind her of home. Sarah doesn't trust 'the whole "No Frills" thing'. She says 'I tend to go with the brands I know.' The dishwashing liquid mum always used can sate a Y consumer's powerful need for family warmth—especially when she is renting a sparsely furnished studio apartment. It is amazing how artfully the brands have managed to associate quality and reliability with a logo. An ad with a cool guy wearing a Rip Curl shirt isn't going to make Daniel go out and buy that product. But if it came down to a choice between a recognised brand and one he didn't know, he'd go with a brand name because 'it's reputable and you know it's going to last'. Yers say they aren't stuck on a brand but do want products that are 'nice', 'well-designed', 'good quality', 'long-lasting' and 'reliable'. But ultimately all these qualities equate in their mind with products that are branded.

In addition to these nostalgic forms of brand loyalty and assumptions about quality, there is a strong tendency amongst Y consumers to conform to the spending habits of their friendship group. Because Y consumers are so cynical about advertising and corporations, they are difficult to market to. And so corporations and their advertisers attempt to harness the most important element of Y culture in marketing to this cohort—friendship. Whilst Yers' brand loyalties are brittle, their loyalty to their friends is strong. Word of mouth and personal recommendations from friends are highly influential, and so they are likely to follow trends rather than just brands. Trends seem to be driven in part by the choices of those around them, rather than being forced on Yers from above by corporate message makers. The difficulty for marketers is that these trends come and go in often unpredictable ways, created as they are out of a dynamic interaction between social, cultural and economic forces.[31]

Recognising friendship as a driving factor in youth consumption has encouraged marketers to develop new technologies such as peer-to-peer marketing and viral advertising.[32] This, combined with marketing via the Internet, email and text, has created a new advertising culture that combines Y devotion to friendship and love of technology. And so, despite the fact that advertisers know that Y consumers aren't easily fooled into buying stuff, they also know that these same consumers want desperately to belong. Marketers know that it's the fear of not belonging that drives the youth market. As Chris Watt comments in his report on youth and cool, fitting in is 'by far one of the most pressing issues confronting [Gen-Yers] in daily life'.[33] As Pocock and Clarke found, the cost of being different, of not belonging or keeping up with the consumer habits of your peers, is high. You risk social and professional alienation and personal unhappiness. In an uncertain and difficult world, Yers are deciding to fit in rather than stand out. And buying into consumer culture is one way of fitting in.

Against this backdrop of Y consumer conformism, there exists a dedicated albeit small group of Y resisters who practise a new politics of anti-consumerism and anti-corporatism. These resisters have reacted badly to the excessive marketing they have been subjected to since early childhood. Vince Mitchell, Professor of Marketing at the Cass Business School in London, argues that these young people 'show high levels of marketing cynicism, are uninterested in shopping and fashion and practise forms of marketing resistance'.[34] In their Australian-based work, Pocock and Clarke found a significant minority of young people held 'anti-market and anti-fashion attitudes' and 'pursue less fashionable forms of consumption' as a result.[35] As political actors, these young people are willing to exercise their consumer power to make a point, boycotting certain products for ethical reasons.[36] Claire is clearly in the anti-brand minority of Generation Y. In many ways she is an atypical Y girl. She is closer to her mother than her friends, a late bloomer sexually and intensely focused on her humanities degree. She describes herself as 'consciously not brand conscious', recognising that a conscious effort has to be made to resist the pull of branded culture. She sees her peers who walk around with logos visibly displayed on their clothes as 'free billboards for corporations'. If a label is visible on an outfit she is wearing, she will cut it off.

Young people like Claire demonstrate Alissa Quart's belief that Yers 'have not taken the merchandising of their minds, bodies and subjectivities lightly' and are 'willing to fight back'.[37] Some of these resisters have decided to fight back in a more collective and public fashion. They have joined together to create a political movement of culture-jammers and anti-brand activists, who create media space and art that turns the power of the logo against the companies that create and sustain them. *Adbusters* magazine features faux-ads that pierce the corporate veil to reveal the truth about the products being flogged: a drooping bottle of Absolut with the byline 'Absolut Impotence', Calvin Klein style ads with a man peeping into his jocks and a young girl bent over a toilet.[38] The culture-jam movement is connected to the broader anti-globalisation and anti-corporatisation movements, who organise Reclaim the Street events and protests around WTO meetings and other global economic leader forums. These movements, owned and operated by the young, are indicative of a Y politics that has both a global and a local dimension, with a dominant focus on economic inequality and injustice. These resisters illustrate the power of branded culture even more clearly than the packs of label-hungry teens and 20-somethings I encounter trawling through my local shopping mall on the weekend. Generation Y protesters and culture-jammers, as well as individuals like Claire, are reacting to what they perceive to be the more insidious forces that threaten to utterly colonise their world and their future. The intensity with which they state their opinions and pursue their goals is further evidence of the power of consumerism and the dominance of branded culture within the Y world.

It is easy to diagnose Yers' investment in consumption as evidence of their superficiality. But, in fact, their attitudes to consumerism are complex, a knot of contradictions. They are brand conscious but not brand loyal. They believe in their own power as consumers and as the adjudicators of cool. Yet they are heavily influenced by the consumer habits of their friends and family and the endorsement of celebrities. Yers don't like obvious forms of label chasing or naked attempts by advertisers to manipulate them into buying the latest, supposedly must-have product. Yet they believe brands symbolise something important. Brands reflect a sense of security and reliability but also excitement and glamour. Brands shape your identity and can help you project a new identity. Yers believe the brand you wear says something about who you are and who you want to be.

Yers are deeply implicated in the culture of consumption and the brand but, paradoxically, they are also deeply disturbed by the extent to which both dominate their culture. Some worry about the empty, wasteful and superficial nature of corporatism and consumerism and have formed a political movement to combat it. Yet despite all the complications and contradictions in Y attitudes to consumption and branded culture, there is an overwhelming and undiminished desire amongst this group to spend and to spend on branded items. Yers know that their status as voters or workers, homeowners or parents amounts to little when compared with their power as consumers. In the absence of any increased political or social power for this generation, it will continue to see the sphere of consumption as a place to develop personal identity, connect with friends, make choices, influence others and dictate terms.

CHAPTER 10

The searching thing
»

IT'S A FRIDAY NIGHT and I am headed to Hillsong Church's city-based campus. Hillsong is a Pentecostal, evangelical-style church, which over the past decade has grown into a national phenomenon, attracting more than 18 000 people to its Sydney services each week.[1] Tonight I am an expectant tourist at 'Powerhouse', a rock-concert-slash-praise-and-prayer-session catering specifically to ages 18 to 25. The Hillsong website describes Powerhouse as an opportunity to relive those childhood feelings that 'you were born to do something great . . . born to make a difference'.[2] The site explains 'Powerhouse is the friendships that give you the courage to live big. It is discovering the truth about JESUS and sharing it with our mates.'

I have dressed as youthfully as possible but I am not fooling anyone that I am under 25. I approach the church doors just as one of Hillsong's courtesy buses, which ferries its congregation from the universities and Central train station, pulls up. Countless well-dressed and eager Yers climb out of the mini van. Walking through the throng of young people outside is like navigating the entrance to a nightclub. Inside, the atmosphere fits that description nicely. The room is full of more than a hundred hip and trendy teens and 20-somethings. There is pounding music, a fusion of rock, funk and reggae. It's like walking into a Benetton advertisement. Girls and guys from all ethnic backgrounds socialise in groups. Flags from different countries hang from the ceiling. There are scented candles on the tables and chairs, which are arranged to imitate a cafe. Inside the enormous hall where the service will take place, young people are busily setting up, moving chairs and couches, testing the sound equipment for the band that will presumably pound out Hillsong's record-breaking Christian rock. These young people are organised and energetic. Within ten minutes of my arrival, one of them approaches me and introduces herself. She is hyper-friendly and looks like she could be a sales assistant at Sportsgirl. Suddenly I feel about 50 years old and am getting cold feet about staying for the show. 'I should come back for a service with older people,' I tell her. 'You can stay if you want,' the young woman tells me. 'You're going to love Powerhouse—it's awesome!'

Hillsong is succeeding in attracting a good-sized Y congregation, whilst the more traditional religious communities have taken on the aura of a convalescent home. Young people in Pentecostal churches like Hillsong now account for 30 per cent of all church-going young Australians, double the proportion that the Catholic and Anglican faiths attract.[3] Hillsong-style churches are crowd-pleasers too, with satisfaction amongst active members in the 15–25 age bracket highest among the Pentecostal denominations and lowest among followers of the Catholic Church.[4] This success is in part due to the image Hillsong projects. The Yers at the

Powerhouse event were totally unlike the daggy Christians I recall from my university days. The Hillsong services are loud and boisterous, full of joy and excitement, colour and movement. As one Hillsonger writes on the website, the church is 'funky and full of fun [and] always has something exciting on'.

Hillsong's success can also be attributed to the array of youth-specific services it provides. It holds campus events, including beach parties with volleyball and barbecues. Its Connect Groups provide constant social interaction, harnessing the power of friendship so vital to Yers. You can travel with Hillsong on sponsored tours of the United States and Canada to visit like-minded churches. Hillsong provides its congregation with assistance that goes beyond the usual counselling and care. It runs budgeting and business courses, weight-loss and fitness classes, job creation and business mentoring, and leadership seminars. Hillsong assists its congregation with maintaining their careers and lifestyles as much (if not more) as their inner spirituality.

But the real key to Hillsong's success with the Y demographic is the message. Hillsong theology gestures towards tolerance and flexibility in an effort to be in sync with Y attitudes to life. Brian Houston, the church leader, on the Hillsong website, states that his unique teachings have a 'commitment to inclusion and understanding'. Houston says, 'Sadly, the Church is often seen to be always imposing their view on the world. Being relevant requires us not to be judgmental, but rather seeing the world with understanding and moved with compassion.'[5]

Hillsong theology is also overwhelmingly positive, which gels nicely with the Y generation's confidence and enthusiasm. The term 'evangelical' derives from 'evangel' or 'good news'.[6] And the Hillsong message is all about good news. Traditional religions like Catholicism preach that if you are good in this life, you will be rewarded after you die. But Hillsongers aren't prepared to wait that long. Hillsong teaches that if you love God, you will be rewarded in this life as well. Gone is the poverty aspect of the conventional religions. Houston preaches that through God, there is not just spiritual abundance available but also cold, hard cash. In the 'Prayer and Praise' section of the website, one Hillsonger writes 'After 10 years of renting, saving and believing in God, we have finally bought our first house in Sydney!' Another Hillsonger testifies 'Praise God for the Youth Ministry of Hillsong Church—specifically eight [Hillsongers] who blessed my son for his 17th birthday with a brand new X-BOX! He had the best birthday ever!'

Which makes me wonder if maybe this birthday boy had loved God even more, would he have scored an iPod as well? The genius of the Hillsong message, especially in relation to its Y audience, is that the more negative, self-sacrificial aspects of Christianity have been underplayed in favour of a more self-centred, materialistic approach. In his essay on the contemporary appeal of religious fundamentalism, Hugh Mackay argues that the current popularity of churches like Hillsong is connected to 'two of our national preoccupations: the growing emphasis on me—self-discovery, self-absorption, self-indulgence—and the closely connected embrace of materialism'.[7]

The success of churches like Hillsong with young people stands in stark relief against a backdrop of general agnosticism and a decline in support for the traditional churches. Only 5 per cent of young adults attend church regularly.[8] While 61 per cent of the total population never attends church, the figure rises to 68 per cent amongst 18–29-year-olds.[9] Nearly one in five young people aged 15 to 24 say they have no religion, a similar rate to that amongst 25–34-year-olds (with the rate for both groups being higher than in any other age group).[10] Market researcher Marc L'Huillier states that religion regularly ends up at the bottom of the priority list of those young Australians who are interviewed for the annual Spin Sweeney Youth Report.[11]

How can we account for this broad-based rejection and disinterest in religion? Even though many Yers went to private schools with religious foundations, they recall church services and religious education as really, really boring. They are the equivalent of overcooked vegetables—something forced upon you in childhood to the point where you develop a lifelong aversion. The feeling that religion is boring has also been reinforced by the general secularisation of our society, a movement pioneered by the Boomers. Hugh Mackay observes that it was the Boomers that fronted the mass exodus from the traditional churches. They were proud and sometimes vitriolic 'in their resistance to organised religion'.[12] This rubbed off on their offspring. For example, Liam was born into a Catholic family, went to a Catholic primary school and attended church until he was 14. He left the church in his mid-teens because he stopped seeing Catholicism as a 'worthwhile way to be spiritual'. No wonder. His father was a Catholic priest for 20 years but left in the late 1970s. His mother still attends church but is 'furious about how the Church is run these days, how repressive the culture of her church is and how horrible the archbishop is'. Jim has 'absolutely no belief' in religion, an attitude inherited from his father. He says 'My dad found it hard to accept the Vatican's endorsement of the war on Vietnam and rebelled against the stifling moral atmosphere of his Catholic upbringing; so I guess I was socialised to be highly suspicious of organised religion.' Even some religious parents like Karen's have taught their children to question orthodoxy. Karen considers herself religious but her religious commitment is a considered one. 'My parents have taught me not to blindly accept anything,' she says, 'so I have put a lot of thought into my religion, trying to figure out why I believe what I believe.'

The conventional churches have done much to erode their own integrity in the eyes of all believers, especially younger ones. Yers grew up in a time when many priests and clergy were found guilty of the sexual abuse of children (and were protected by the church hierarchy despite their sins). The hypocrisy of the church has undermined its moral authority and Yers take a dim view of being lectured to on ethics by an institution they see as corrupt. Caroline, a 21-year-old public servant, has no interest in listening to 'a bunch of people with double standards'. She says 'The exact same people who believe that abortion is wrong have sex with little boys.' In his opinion piece on religion, (focused mostly on Catholicism) Simon Castles tells us that his general 'distrust of authority figures' was further confirmed when so many priests were exposed as paedophiles. His suspicion of priests is 'further heightened by the vow of celibacy they must take'. Castles writes 'That these men believe they are in a position to offer marriage counselling and family planning advice to the community frankly borders on the ludicrous.' The discrimination against women and homosexuals as practised by the organised religions is also a major turn-off for Yers. As Castles comments, 'I wouldn't accept being part of a school, a university, a club or a workplace that treats women and gays as second-class citizens, so why would I be part of a church that does?'[13] Yers are highly suspicious of the hierarchical and authoritarian nature of the traditional religions. They question the motives of religious leaders. Despite his strong Catholic roots, Lawrence sees religion as 'potentially evil'. He says 'I find it hard to put much faith in religion. I think a lot of people exploit religion for their own purposes by taking advantage of people who are vulnerable.' And so in Y eyes, the churches have joined corporations and governments on the growing list of 'big institutions you can't trust'.

The tarnished reputation of 'Big Religion' and their parents' rejection of the religious life has left Yers largely bereft of any spiritual direction. As they were growing up, Yers didn't even have a definite moral framework to reject, let alone follow. Society has not yet come up with anything adequate to fill this void left by the decline of organised religions. But that void still exists and its persistence explains in part the interest amongst Yers in spirituality. In his work on school leavers, Hugh Mackay observes that while 'no one seems to like being called "religious" . . . spirituality is a really, really interesting subject'.[14] Even though Yers like Claire 'don't believe in the existence of God' and have drifted away from the religion they grew up in, they still understand 'the need to be part of a spiritual group that helps us create meaning in our lives'. Liselle is 'not a religious person', but still sees faith as important because 'it gives us a sense of belonging and understanding'. Arya went to a Catholic high school but her parents are both Buddhists. Whilst she doesn't believe in organised religion, she does empathise with those who yearn to be included in a community, 'which they don't feel included in outside a church'.

Arya understands the need to belong, to share meaning about the things that don't make sense in life, the need for answers to the important questions. She knows religious communities can provide loving support and sees that as admirable. In fact she would like to see those values brought into secular society.

This interest in 'things spiritual' expresses itself in various ways. A significant proportion of young people are interested in exploring 'alternative' or non-Western religions like Buddhism, which already counts many Yers amongst its adherents.[15] Certainly these religions are exotic and different, with celebrity followers and high profile leaders. But more importantly, Buddhism seems to attract Yers for its non-authoritarian quality and the chance for self-discovery it offers. Sarah is 22 years old and comes from a well-off family in the northern suburbs of Sydney. She isn't religious but her 'big thing' at the moment is self-help books. When we met for coffee, she had just finished *The Art of Happiness* by the Dalai Lama. I reminded her that the Dalai Lama was more like the Pope than Dr Phil, but that didn't seem to bother her. Sarah defines her idea of religion as:

> ... *more about how you think about things, how you go about your life to change things to be how you want them to be, rather than someone sitting up in the sky telling you what's going to happen. It's about taking control of things yourself, shaping things the way you want them.*

Similarly, there is a broad interest (not just amongst Yers) in healthy lifestyles, yoga, meditation, astrology, psychic readings, tarot cards, angel-worship, popular paganism in the form of witchcraft and occult practices—all these interests have a spiritual dimension that offers inspiration, peace, guidance and a belief in something bigger and more profound than the tangible world around us. Ruth Webber, an expert on young people and spirituality, observes that Yers adopt an organic and eclectic approach to their search for spiritual meaning, one that attempts to escape 'the confines of formal organisations' and rigid hierarchies. However, Webber also found that the fact that their beliefs and practices are often inconsistent 'does not appear to bother' Yers in the least.[16]

This concern for the spiritual amongst a generation famous for its drive to consume, have fun and live for the moment seems contradictory. But this is a contradictory generation, called Generation Paradox by some market researchers. But their interest in fun and material goods doesn't negate the fact that for Yers something is missing, namely more effective ways to work out the big questions in life. How do I live? How do I make decisions? What's it all about? Hard work made even harder by the fact that this generation, like X, grew up in a time when ethical decisions were, according to Eckersley, 'less of a social given and more a matter of personal choice'.[17] Hugh Mackay agrees that both X and Y were raised 'without having had a moral framework clearly espoused and unambiguously articulated by their parents'.[18] Courtesy of secularism, they have grown up with a flexible and tolerant approach to decision-making and life choices. Courtesy of post-modernism, they occupy a world which Eckersley describes as 'characterized by ambivalence, ambiguity, relativism, pluralism, fragmentation and contingency'.[19] Mackay also found that for the vast majority of Yers, 'notions of moral absolutes' are 'as alien as the idea of rigid gender distinctions'.[20] So they don't bother searching for them. Rather, the quest is for personal fulfilment and truth on your own terms, what Coupland calls 'personal taboos'. In *Generation X* he writes that these are 'small rules for living . . . that allow one to cope with everyday life in the absences of cultural or religious dictums'.[21] In formulating these 'personal taboos', the example of the parents is an early and crucial influence.[22] Yers like Sarah, a 21-year-old business student, nominate siblings, friends and the media as persuasive also. Tony gets his direction in life 'from everywhere—family, friends, movies, culture'. For others, overseas work and travel holds out the possibility that a change of context and new challenges will deliver insight and personal growth.

But ultimately, in the search for meaning and purpose, Yers have been left to fend for themselves. This situation is ironic when we consider the amount of energy and money that has been spent guiding and regulating Y lives. As American journalist David Brook observes: 'When it comes to character and virtue, the most mysterious area of all, suddenly the laissez-faire ethic rules: You're on your own, Jack and Jill; go figure out what is true and just for yourselves.'[23] On the question of spirituality and ethics, Yers have basically been left to their own devices. They have had to develop their own moral codes and values without the direct guidance of parents, mentors, employers or role models.[24]

Consumption, the pursuit of material things, is clearly not enough to provide Yers with a reason to live. Whilst young people want money for the freedom and options it provides, most recognise it can't be the basis for a life philosophy. Paul, a lawyer in training, says 'I try not to let my life choices be driven by the desire for lots of money because I know it doesn't really satisfy me at all.' Yers question the values of a society that equates success with money. Tim knows that our society defines success as having 'a big car, bigger house, biggest mortgage payed off on an enormous salary'. He also believes this success is often accompanied by 'two divorces, two children in child care, two minutes' free time in the week'. Meg agrees, saying that our society defines success by 'the size of your house and how good you car is'. In her opinion, 'It should be about how happy you are, how great a mum or dad you are, that you work at a great job which you like.' (Meg and Tim's views reflect a deeper questioning both of the values of our society but also the choices and lifestyles of their parents.) In their studies of youth and consumption, Pocock and Clarke found that while young people 'enjoy having material goods, they are sharply critical of those with "too much" and see them as greedy, socially inauthentic and poorly equipped for later life'.[25] Many Yers are looking beyond material things for a fulfilled existence.

In the absence of a definite way forward, the options for living—what career, which boyfriend, where to live, when to marry and have kids—are seemingly endless. But all this choice creates its own problems. Yers often feel overwhelmed and bewildered by the seemingly endless array of choices available to them. Mary Jane, for example, believes that the world presents her peers with 'too many options'. When I interviewed David about his future plans, the usually

articulate and opinionated 25-year-old was flummoxed:

> *I wish I could map goals in a more comprehensive fashion so I could answer your question about what I am going to be doing in a year or three years or five years. Do I want to work overseas? Should we pay off the bulk of our mortgage before we have kids? If there is a sense of unease, it is because there are so many things I could and want to do.*

Education and confidence have given Yers freedom and opportunity in terms of career, living arrangements, relationships and so on. Whilst according to Coupland the 'variety can be intoxicating', it can also lead to what he calls 'option paralysis', 'the tendency, when given unlimited choices, to make none'.[26] Y columnist Rachel Hills argues that with such a smorgasbord of 'choice' on offer, it can be hard for Yers to make up their minds, especially about the bigger, harder decisions.[27] For some Yers struggling to make sense of life, too many options can be as bad as too few.

The hard task of making life decisions is made even harder by the typical Y lifestyle, which is one of constant movement and pressure to achieve. As both kids and teens, Yers were pushed by their parents and teachers to always be busy and successful. They spent their childhood years in structured, adult-organised activities. Growing up in a middle-class family and privately educated, Martin felt this pressure to always be on the move:

> *My whole generation had our after-school regime booked up with sport or cadets or chess. Anything to keep us busy. Our headmaster's philosophy was 'keep the boys busy during adolescence and they won't realise they are going through it'. While I see his point, we lived like pretend adults.*

But even as adults, Yers have continued to keep this frenetic pace. They always feel the need to be doing, achieving, socialising, travelling, buying new stuff, changing and learning. Howe and Strauss argue that Yers feel 'a growing sense of urgency about what they have to do to achieve their personal and group goals' and that 'pressure is what keeps them constantly in motion—moving, busy, purposeful, without nearly enough hours in the day to get it all done.'[28] In his observations of elite American college students, David Brooks comes to the same conclusion. The Yers he met 'lead a frenetic, tightly packed existence', which was 'structured, supervised and stuffed with enrichment'. Brooks found that these young Americans were so busy and overwhelmed they couldn't even find the time or energy to put into 'real relationships'.[29] Brendon, 22, feels the same way as Brook's Ivy League students. 'Life is too busy to fit in relationships,' Brendon says. 'They are too much work. The ability to commit to something is difficult in an age where we are supposed to have instant reactions, where life is a kaleidoscope of new experiences.'

As a result, many Yers worry about the toll which all this pressure to succeed has on personal relationships. For example, Arya values relationships but wonders about the impact her ambition and desire for success will have on her capacity to maintain them. She says:

> I want to plan out my life so that I can prioritise relationships with the people I love. But that is really difficult when you want to succeed. You have to take your work past a comfortable level, work ridiculous hours and push yourself intellectually and physically to achieve a result.

All this leaves Yers with little time for deeper thinking, an essential prerequisite for working out the bigger picture, exploring issues of meaning and purpose, all those things they seem to yearn for. Howe and Strauss claim that nothing in the average Y existence 'stimulates self-reflection'.[30] There are, however, thoughtful Yers like Antony who recognise they will have to slow down in order to work out some of life's trickier questions. Antony feels that one of the important issues for Generation Y is time:

> *More and more, we keep expecting things to happen the second after it is asked for. You just look it up on the Net and you find it in 30 seconds. That creates an expectation that everything should happen quickly. That's not a great way for the world to function. Stopping and thinking about something can also be valuable.*

With all the challenges facing Yers—pressure, stress, uncertainty and infinite choice—how are they faring? Are they happy? If the usual social indicators of wellbeing are to be believed—drug abuse, suicide rates, mental illness, risk-taking behaviours—then Yers are much happier than their Gen X counterparts. Howe & Strauss state that in the United States Generation X 'grew up as the kids whose low test scores and high rates of crime, suicide, and substance abuse marked a post-war extreme for American youth'.[31] During the 1980s and 1990s, when Australian Xers were in their teens and early 20s, suicide became a major public health issue, especially for young men. Drug abuse amongst young people also became a serious concern during this period. By contrast, Yers are a happy, well-behaved and optimistic bunch. In a 2003 report on the health and wellbeing of young Australians, it was found that the vast majority declare they are 'delighted, pleased or mostly satisfied with their lives'.[32] This is a healthy demographic, reporting low levels of psychological distress. After peaking in 1997, the suicide rate for young people has fallen.[33] Drug abuse, smoking and risky sexual behaviours have also dropped.[34]

But this is only part of the picture. Whilst smoking and drug use is down, alcohol use and binge drinking has increased since 1992, with girls keeping up with boys in patterns of alcohol abuse.[35] This generation has also seen a rise in the use and abuse of prescription medicine. A recent parliamentary inquiry into the misuse of prescription drugs found evidence of 'selling, swapping and sharing prescription drugs or medication' amongst young people.[36] Certainly Yers are the first generation to be heavily subscribed drugs such as Ritalin, anti-depressants and other drugs to combat conditions such as acne and obesity.[37] Gone are the days when it was okay to be a depressed, distracted, slightly overweight teen with some transitory skin problems. In a world where the pressure to be well-adjusted, successful and good-looking is ever more intense, medicine can intervene to get rid of those afflictions usually seen as synonymous with young adulthood.[38]

And whilst much fanfare has accompanied the falling rate of youth suicide in Australia, we still have one of the highest rates in the developed world. Many Yers know someone their age who has attempted or committed suicide.[39] When asked why their contemporaries might consider suicide, Yers nominate a lack of direction, a failing sense of purpose and hope. Even though 23-year-old Greg is funny and smart, with a steady job and friends, he still gets depressed when he starts thinking about how 'lost' he is. Thoughts about suicide creep in when he dwells on his sense of 'hopelessness' and 'not knowing what to do'. His friend Simon also reveals that he sometimes wonders 'What's the point?'. He says 'It is easy to get upset if you put a lot of effort into something and it doesn't work out. Then you think, what else is there to look forward to, what else is there worth living for?' Meisha grew up in a rural area, where young people are at a particularly high risk of suicidal behaviour. She believes that her peers who have committed suicide or attempted it were 'unhappy and unsettled about life and where it was heading or not heading'.

On these critical questions of life purpose and direction, the parent generation and society in general has failed this emerging generation of adults. Yers are adamant that neither workaholism nor materialism can suffice as a philosophy for living. Whilst their parents have given them enough education and opportunity to open up a hundred options in terms of their careers, they haven't provided the tools or guidelines via which Yers can forge a clear path towards happiness and fulfilment. Now wonder they are searching around, like magpies, picking up a disparate collection of truths and rituals in order to find some kind of ethical and emotional state of peace.

Generation Y has always lived with pressure and high expectations. Whilst their optimism and energy is hard to curtail, they are still susceptible to the kinds of problems Xers faced as young adults—despair, lack of direction, depression and suicidal thoughts. Few see traditional religion as the path to working out these issues. Unconventional churches like Hillsong are more successful in attracting Y attention for the fun, lifestyle support and community they provide. But those who find guidance and solace in religion are still in the minority. The majority of young people have been left on their own to sort out life's bigger questions. As a consequence, they are taking a DIY approach to spirituality, adopting and discarding a variety of practices and beliefs in the process.

Some, like Tony, are 'just floating along', happy to admit they have 'no idea what it is all about'. A small group—the ones I worry about most—are struggling. These are the ones who have fallen or may fall through the cracks into self-harm and long-term drug abuse. For them the 'searching thing' seems an impossible task.

CHAPTER 11

The future's so bright,
I gotta wear shades
»

TALKING ABOUT THE FUTURE is a challenging task for people
of any age. But when it comes to Generation Y, the question
of where its members are going, what they plan to do with
their lives, is about as palatable as a week-old pizza. And I'm
not talking about ten or twenty years hence. For most of them
'the future' is five years. And many don't even feel capable
of surmising where they might be then. Most question the
validity of even asking questions about the future. Amongst
the Yers I spoke to, Meisha, a 23-year-old medical student,
has 'no idea' where she will be in five years' time because she
doesn't think 'that far ahead' (although presumably she will
still be finishing her medical degree). Kristy tries to 'go with
the flow' and not live too much in the future. Trudi says 'I
don't tend to think 20, 30, 40 years down the track. The future
is the next couple of years.' Naturally this unwillingness or
inability to talk about anything beyond next year's birthday
celebrations is part of the luxury of youth. But it is also symp-
tomatic of an uncertain world where planning far in advance
is reliant on things staying stable, people being reliable and

the world remaining the same. Generation Y knows that's both unrealistic and boring.

Yers resist getting specific about their plans for the rest of their 20s. Despite this, their feelings about the future are largely positive, a sharp contrast to the youthful attitudes of their predecessors. One of Generation X's defining characteristics was its pessimism. We were consumed with what Douglas Coupland calls 'a mood of darkness and inevitability', a terrible sense of 'futurelessness'.[1] Yers are blindingly optimistic about their own future possibilities for success and happiness. For example, Louisa feels her future has 'a really nice glow' to it. She says 'I have worked really hard and I am enjoying where I am now. Why wouldn't I feel good about the future?' Scott is also confident, saying, 'I really do feel good about the future. I don't feel like there is anything not to be optimistic about.' Jackie is 'definitely optimistic' about a future with 'a great career, family and happiness'. David is sure that 'life holds out for me a whole stack of things that are going to be fun and exciting'. According to Brooks, this generation have mostly known 'parental protection, prosperity and peace'.[2] This was demonstrated by many of the Yers I interviewed who observed that there hadn't been any 'major issues' that have threatened the way people their age live. And so young people believe (with a mixture of youthful naiveté and Y enthusiasm) that these good times will continue regardless.

In conversations about the future, social researchers often find people are confident about their own direction but worried about the fate of the world at large. Xers were unlike previous youth cohorts in this regard. We felt our futures were profoundly implicated in the downward slide into economic savagery and environmental degradation that we were certain was coming. Yers are more typical of the researchers' findings in that they have, as 23-year-old Jenny describes, 'a personal optimism but a larger pessimism'. This 'larger pessimism' is the consequence of concerns about, amongst other things, terrorism, environmental problems and the growing gap between rich and poor. But underneath this list of international worries exists a more profound belief that humankind will find solutions to the problems that have been created. Even though Steve is concerned about the environment, he is certain that 'science and medicine will keep getting better'. James is an actuary for an insurance company. Calculating future risks is part of his job and he is supremely confident that the immediate future is secure. He says 'At work we have been doing studies on where the world will be in twenty years. It looks like nothing is really going to change that drastically.' Daniel believes it is easy to be pessimistic but:

> *For some reason, people always think the future will be bleak. People don't write books about the future and how great it is going to be! I don't think we are headed in the right direction now but that doesn't mean it isn't going to change. I've always loved history because I find comfort in the fact that there is a cycle where bad things don't last. By the time I'm old, the world is going to be very different.*

Popular culture has registered this belief that humankind will prevail against the odds. In the disaster movies of the Y years—films like *Deep Impact, Terminator III—Judgement Day, The Day After Tomorrow* and *War of the Worlds*—the resounding message is that human ingenuity, determination and technological know-how will combine to ensure the survival of the species. Part of this Y confidence about the future also rests on the fact that Yers live in a stable and prosperous democracy. Most of the Yers I spoke to feel secure in Australia, a place many of them call 'the best country in the world'.

Despite these basic feelings of optimism, Generation Y knows it will face some hardships and difficulties in the coming years. The primary and dominant concern is economic. In its 'Consultations with Young Australians', the Business Council of Australia found that the average 25-year-old nominates housing affordability, financial security and unemployment as their top concerns for the future.[3] Yers are entering the workforce knowing there is no such thing as job security. They know a university degree will guarantee debt but not a quality job. Daniel is almost blithely aware that his career choice in journalism will ensure he will be out of work for periods of his life. He says 'That's just something I am going to have to deal with.' Sophie would like to have bought a house by the time she's 30 but seriously doubts whether that will happen. Yers are entering adulthood with a sneaking suspicion they might be paying rent forever.

On top of these financial strictures, Yers are looking ahead to the time when their parents retire and age. The Business Council of Australia found that young people believe managing our ageing population will be one of the greatest challenges in the next two decades, up there with the environment and Australia's position in the world. David is 25, married with a mortgage and thinking about having kids. He knows that his generation are 'going to pay for our parents to grow old gracefully' and calls it 'a massive burden'. Many Yers have more than a sneaking suspicion that under current conditions they are economically screwed. The Boomers have the property market cornered. After paying off substantial education debts, Y taxes will go to ensuring their long-living parents are looked after. Where is the financial breathing space needed to establish an adult life, something Yers are constantly chastised for resisting?

Gen-Yers are also publicly criticised for their sense of entitlement and self-interest, especially by older managers and university teachers. This is the generation who has had to pay for everything, who have been brought up in a user-pays world. In contrast, their parents had a free education, knew a supportive social services and health care system, and enjoyed an early working life of relative stability and promise. No wonder Y has adopted a survival of the fittest attitude to life, always demanding value for money, with a constant eye on what's in it for them. They are moving forward and trying to succeed in a world where governments, corporations and other social institutions provide little support and even less guidance.

In talking to Yers about their future worries, contradictions emerge, as always. Concern about their own material wellbeing is mixed up with a belief that unchecked consumerism and waste has to stop. In its consultations, the Business Council found that young Australians didn't believe 'materialism and hedonism' were a worthy substitute to meaningful spirituality or a sense of purpose in life. Arya, a 22-year-old arts graduate, believes that in the next 30 years, 'our lives are going to have to change'. She says 'In Australia we have had such a privileged existence. As a generation, we have had such an abundant and selfish lifestyle. That can't go on forever.'

Connected to this general feeling amongst Yers that life isn't all career and money is the issue of work/family balance. They want the opportunity to maintain friend-ships, build meaningful relationships that can lead to marriage and most of all have children. But there is so much to do and experience before then. And the question of how all this can be achieved financially is almost unfathomable. Despite the recent public panic over the falling birth rate, there is no current indication that Yers will reverse this trend by having children earlier. Fifty years ago, mothers in their early 20s were the norm. Now the biggest group giving birth are women aged 30 to 34.[4] Young women under 25 years give birth to only one in five of all babies born in Australia, and teenage birth rates are generally low.[5] Whilst the overwhelm-ing majority of Yers want children, their expectations may well be disappointed by biology, economics, bad luck or uninformed choices.[6]

As Xers have already found, the conflicting timetables of men and women will continue to cause stress in relation-ships between the sexes, especially when it comes to having children. There is a small but significant age gap between X mothers and fathers; the average age for first-time mothers in 2001 was 30, whereas the average age for first-time fathers was 32. Some Y men even nominate 40 as a good age to be a father, a time when they see themselves capable of taking on the economic responsibilities involved in supporting a family. As we already know, few 40-year-old women conceive easily. Seeing the pain of infertility and childlessness amongst their older sisters, Y girls have known at an early age that you shouldn't leave these things too late. They are likely to have some kind of timeline for their personal life—married at 28, first kid at 30, etc. Unfortunately for the girls, Y men don't want to work to these timetables. And so, as with the clash over work and family responsibilities, Y men and women are headed for further grief over when to commit and, more importantly, when to parent. Those with bad timing or cold feet will fuel the expected upward trend in people living alone.[7]

Signs also point to the trend in small families continuing. Whilst 'postponed' parenting is one of the reasons Yers will head up small families, economic and lifestyle factors also play a part. In fact, it seems the dominant force of 'lifestyle' is enough to dictate even the most personal and intimate decisions a Y couple might make. For example, whilst Renee comes from a big Lebanese family, two kids of her own is more than enough. She says:

> I don't want more than two kids because then there are concerns about maintaining quality of life. More than three and you have to get a Tarago! While my parents raised four kids on less money than we have now, our lifestyle choices are different. We still want the lifestyle and the holidays and the family.

Being born Y has always been full of contradictions. On the one hand, Yers have been nurtured and protected. On the other they have been subject to intense pressure to succeed. They are highly educated, with big dreams and huge expectations. But in making important choices about their careers and their lives, they are more often than not rudderless, without any firm ethical framework or life purpose to guide them. These factors combine to ensure that a good proportion of Yers are headed for what is termed a 'quarterlife crisis'. This is a kind of emotional and career breakdown that occurs in the mid to late 20s, often after the relatively sheltered world of school and university has been left behind. The American website *Quarterlife Crisis* offers counselling to those suffering from this very 21st century affliction:

> *Having trouble adjusting to the 'real world' after twentysomething years in school? You are NOT alone. Surprisingly, this often traumatic transition has NEVER been studied before. But it is real, and it can often be scary. People often find that school has not prepared them to face the challenges of the 'real world'. There are career options, financial responsibilities, and social adjustments we never even considered in the sheltered environment of college campuses.[8]*

Many Yers, used to the direction, drive and support offered at school and at home, are floundering amidst a sea of choice, opportunity and reality. This often leaves them 'unsettled, stressed, anxious, and all too often, depressed'.[9] Yers going through a quarterlife crisis recognise that the drive for money, material things and success at work isn't enough. They need a broader context for action and decision-making, a sense of meaning and purpose. The quarterlife crisis is beautifully depicted in the recent film *In Good Company*. Carter Duryed, played by Topher Grace, is a highly successful, smart and ambitious Yer. At 26 Carter has everything: the swanky house, a new Porsche, a trophy wife and a big promotion as head of sales in a multinational corporation. But soon after his promotion, everything begins to disintegrate. His wife leaves him, unsure whether she wants children with a workaholic who is never around. He is distanced from his parents and has few visible friends. He can only find time to exercise in the office and plans work meetings on the weekend so he won't feel lonely. But by the end of the film, he has left all this behind to take time for a life re-think, to jog along the beach, to search for a vocation that 'means something', at least to him. The quarterlife crisis may well be a right of passage most Yers must go through in their attempts to balance financial concerns with personal fulfilment, career expectations with emotional needs, and the desire for security with a desire for flexibility and change.

I was inspired to write this book by my own experiences as a teacher, namely the realisation that over a few years a generation gap can emerge between me and those only a decade or so younger. Social and economic change is so constant and quick that generations have been narrowed down to ten-year spans, whereas once at least 30 years separated one generation from the next. Over the course of writing about Generation Y, my feelings about its members— their attitudes, behaviours and way they might change the world—swung back and forth, from admiration to envy, from sympathy to suspicion. That being said, I always loved talking to them and hearing about their lives. Journalist David Brooks found that whilst most Princeton professors were disturbed by the conformism and hectic lifestyles of their young students, they also found them exciting to teach and profoundly trustworthy. 'Young people are wonderful to be around,' writes Brooks.[10] I found the same thing. My connection, however brief at the start, with the Yers I met has been sustained over the course of writing this book, powered along by emails and meetings over coffee.

186

My ultimate enthusiasm for this generation is not exactly shared by everyone in my generation or older. When I've mentioned the topic of my book to people (Xers in particular), they have often been heard mumbling under their breath, 'those selfish, annoying, lazy little upstarts', etc. Boomer writer Bob Ellis lashed out at Yers recently: 'They're always meeting for coffee. They're always on the f**king mobile phone cancelling appointments and rescheduling others. They have very brief sexual adventures before returning to their tight-knit group of friends.'[11] And what's so wrong with all that? I thought Boomers like Ellis pioneered the sexual revolution, where brief sexual encounters were *de rigueur*?

Slowly we are seeing the signs of a new generational war. X against Boomers, Y against Boomers and (more interestingly) X against Y. The generational clashes of the 1960s were over cultural issues and the war in Vietnam. The new generational war will almost certainly be over economics. We are already seeing significant amounts of 'boomer envy' amongst both X and Y. Boomer envy is defined by Coupland as 'that envy of material wealth and long-range material security accrued by older members of the baby boom generation by virtue of fortunate births'.[12] Xers, as they get further away from 30 and closer to 40, are sick of waiting in line for the Boomers to retire from their plum jobs in the public and private sectors. Boomers and Xers, on the other hand, are grappling with a new generation that has very different attitudes to work, sex, time, space, loyalty, commitment and culture. The battles are no longer over who knows how to program the VCR. Yers are downloading an entirely new way of life. The rest of us will have to understand and adapt.

In any generational war, I would put my money on Y. Their knees are still good and they know how to get hold of the drugs that give you stamina. But I don't think that's the way to go. Older generations, X but particularly the Boomers, have created the world Yers are adapting to. And, in turn, we will have to adapt to a world according to Y. There is no doubt that due to its size, energy and talent, Generation Y will shape those areas of society they choose to engage with. Will they fuel the rise and rise of consumption and materialism? Or will they be the first to pioneer a movement towards a new conscious-consumer culture that rejects the brand name and unbridled corporatisation? Will they achieve the right balance between work and family? Or will Y women join their Xer sisters in becoming harried and guilty working mums, struggling with their partners and their employers for a fair deal at home and at work? Will they reject oppressive forms of body fascism, turning their back on cosmetic surgery and submitting to the ageing process gracefully? Or will Botox injections join manicures and haircuts as just another reasonable beauty treatment for the average woman? Will Y boys pioneer new ways to be a man, to father their children? Will they all join together to transform national politics or bypass it altogether to forge a new politics that combines local and global concerns? I have seen the potential in this generation for both radical transformation and terrible conformism. The world according to Y has not yet arrived ... but it is coming. Get ready.

Endnotes
»

Chapter 1

1   Different social researchers nominate various years between 1979 and 1981 as marking the beginning point for Generation Y. Neil Howe and William Strauss, who have written extensively on this generation, choose 1982 and so do I. In this book I focus on the vanguard of Generation Y, those aged between 18 and 25. Neil Howe and William Strauss, *Millennials Rising: The Next Great Generation*, Vintage, New York, 2000, p. 4.

2   George Barna, *Generation Next: What You Need to Know About Today's Youth*, Regal, Ventura, 1995, p. 46.

3   See <www.harrisinteractive.com>.

4   Drake Bennett, 'Doing Disservice', *The American Prospect*, October 2003, p. 20.

5   Robert Cummins, Richard Eckersley, Julie Pallant and Melanie Davern, 'Wellbeing in Australia and the aftermath of September 11', Survey 3, Report 3.1, May 2002, Australian Centre on Quality of Life, Victoria.

6   For Kristen's report see <www.uniya.com.au>.

7   Howe and Strauss, *Millennials Rising*, p. 3.

8   Howe and Strauss, *Millennials Rising*, p. 7.

9   ibid., p. 56.

10 Generation X wasn't the first group to be described in these terms. The Boomers have also been described as the 'Me Generation' proving once again that young people are often labelled selfish by their elders.

11   Hugh Mackay, *Generations: Baby boomers, their parents and their children*, Macmillan, Sydney, 1997, p. 137.

12   Simon Castles, 'Reality Bites Gen X Myth', *The Age*, 22 April 2002.

13   William Strauss and Neil Howe, *Generations: The History of America's Future 1584 to 2069*, William Morrow, New York, 1991, p. 317.

14   Howe and Strauss, *Millennials Rising*, p. 174.

15   Rick Hicks and Kathy Hicks, *Boomers, Xers and Other Strangers: Understanding the Generational Differences that Divide Us*, Tyndale, Illinois, 1999, p. 185.

16   Hugh Mackay, *The Mackay Report: Leaving School*, Report no. 98, March 2000, Sydney, p. 26.

17   Douglas Coupland calls this 'clique maintenance: the need of one generation to see the generation following it as deficient so as to bolster its own collective ego'. Douglas Coupland, *Generation X: Tales for An Accelerated Culture*, St Martin's Press, New York, 1991, p. 21.

18   Ariadne Vromen, 'Three political myths about young people', *The Drawing Board*, <www.econ.usyd.edu.au>, 26 March 2004.

19   Richard Eckersley, *Well and Good: How We Feel & Why It Matters*, Text, Melbourne, 2004, p. 113.

20   Amanda Hodge, 'Generation next rides a wave of optimism', *The Australian*, 8 December, 2004.

21   Jim DeRogatis, 2001, 'What's up with Generation Y?', *Salon*, <www.salon.com> [23 March 2004].

22   See <www.abs.gov.au>.

23   The first wave of Generation Y has 'the lowest child-to-parent ratio in American history'. Strauss and Howe, *Generations*, p. 341.

24   Howe and Strauss, *Millennials Rising*, p. 98.

25   Strauss and Howe, *Generations*, p. 318.

26   Howe and Strauss, *Millennials Rising*, p. 76.

27   ibid., pp. 31–2.

28   Strauss and Howe, *Generations*, p. 320.

29   Ani Wierenga, 'Finding and losing the plot: Storying and the value of listening to young people', *Scottish Journal of Youth Issues*, vol. 4, pp. 9–30, p. 11.

30   AAP, 'Youth put away their mobiles for the sake of friendship', *Sydney Morning Herald*, 8 December 2004.

31   Coupland, *Generation X*, p. 7.

32   Mackay, *Generations*, pp. 137–8.

33   Amy Cooper, '21st Century Tribes', *Sun Herald*, 7 March 2004.

34   Mackay, *Generations*, p. 138.

35   Hicks and Hicks, *Boomers, Xers and Other Strangers*, p. 270.

36   Barna, *Generation Next*, p. 46.

37   Bernard Salt, 'The X, Y factor', *Business Review Weekly*, 16–22
      September 2004.

38   Jim Meskauskas, 'Millennials Surfing: Generation Y Online',
      imediaconnection, 2003, <www.imediaconnection.com> [14 May
      2004].

39   Howe and Strauss, *Millennials Rising*, p. 16.

40   Chris Watt, 'Cool's not cool when marketing to youth', *B & T*,
      2003, <www.bandt.com.au> [11 August 2004].

41   In his article on elite college students, journalist David Brooks
      talked to older faculty members at Princeton who were disturbed
      about Generation Y's eagerness to conform. The 'edgy
      individualists' of the Gen X era have all but disappeared from
      campuses, replaced by 'perky conformists' and 'happy kids'. David
      Brooks, 'The Organization Kid', *The Atlantic Monthly*, April 2002,
      www.theatlantic.com, April 2001.

42   Alissa Quart, *Branded: The buying and selling of teenagers*, Arrow,
      London, 2003, p. 111.

43   Melissa Butcher and Mandy Thomas, 'Situating Youth Cultures',
      Ingenious: Emerging Youth Cultures in Urban Australia, Melissa
      Butcher and Mandy Thomas (eds), Pluto, Sydney, 2003, p. 20.

44   Howe and Strauss, *Millennials Rising*, p. 68.

Chapter 2

1   Douglas Coupland, *Generation X: Tales for An Accelerated Culture*,
     St Martin's Press, New York, 1991, pp. 6, 130.

2   Ethan Watters, *Urban Tribes: A Generation Redefines Friendship,
     Family and Commitment*, Bloomsbury, New York, 2003.

3   Julia Baird, 'Bonds behind myth of the urban tribes', *Sydney
     Morning Herald*, 10 April 2004.

4   Hugh Mackay, *The Mackay Report: Leaving School*, Report No. 98, March 2000, Sydney, p. 7.

5   Hugh Mackay, *Generations: Baby boomers, their parents and their children*, Macmillan, Sydney, 1997, p. 152.

6   AAP, 'Youth "put away their mobiles for the sake of friendship"', *Sydney Morning Herald*, 8 December 2004.

7   Nick Hornby, *About a Boy*, Victor Gollancz, London, 1998, pp. 283–4.

8   Mackay, *Leaving School*, p. 9.

9   Rosalind Wiseman, *Queen Bees and Wannabes: Helping your daughter survive cliques, gossip, boyfriends and other realities of adolescence*, Random House, London, 2003, p. 207.

10   Nikki Gemmell, *The Bride Stripped Bare*, Harper Collins, Sydney, 2003, p. 79.

11   Wiseman, *Queen Bees and Wannabees*, p. 207.

12   Steve Biddulph, *Manhood*, Finch Publishing, Sydney, 1994, p. 3.

13   ibid., p. 176.

14   Wiseman, *Queen Bees and Wannabes*, p. 179.

15   George Barna, *Generation Next: What You Need to Know About Today's Youth*, Regal, Ventura, 1995, p. 46.

16   Melissa Butcher and Mandy Thomas, *Generate: Youth Culture and Migration Heritage in Western Sydney*, Institute for Cultural Research, Penrith, 2001, p. 37.

17   Kirsty Needham, 'Generation Y keys in boomer-sized debt', *Sydney Morning Herald*, 22 November 2003.

18   Mackay, *Leaving School*, p. 7.

Chapter 3

1   Susan Hopkins, *Girl Heroes: The new force in popular culture*, Pluto Press, Sydney, 2002, p. 2.

2   Catharine Lumby, *Bad Girls: The media, sex and feminism in the 90s*, Allen & Unwin, Sydney, 1997, p. 160.

3   Noy Thrupkaew, 'Daughters of the Revolution', *The American Prospect*, October 2003, p. 16.

4   Anne Summers, *Damned Whores and God's Police*, Penguin, Victoria, 1994, pp. 505–28.

5   Kathy Bail, *DIY Feminism*, Allen & Unwin, Sydney, 1996, p. 3.

6   For Bulbeck's findings see <http://www.arts.adelaide.edu.au/socialsciences/people/gls/cbullbeck.html>. This percentage tallies roughly with the conclusions in the 2000 Democrats Youth Poll, which found that only 49 per cent of young Australians believe feminism is relevant to their lives. For Poll results see <www.democrats.org.au>. Bulbeck's comparative study of attitudes of young people about gender issues and the women's movement included the US, Australia, Canada, China, India, Vietnam, Indonesia, Thailand, South Korea and Japan. It was based on questionnaires completed by students in their final year of high school or first year of university over the 1999–2003 period. Interestingly, Bulbeck's research shows young Australian men as unsympathetic about a whole range of gender issues when compared with young men in other countries. Whether this is a consequence of the sample of young men surveyed or some particularly virulent form of male chauvinism present in Australian males is hard to ascertain.

7   Thrupkaew, 'Daughters of the Revolution', p. 24.

8   ibid., p. 16.

9   Steve Biddulph, *Manhood*, Finch Publishing, Sydney, 1994, p. 22.

10   Hopkins, *Girl Heroes*, p. 2.

11   ibid., p. 7.

12   Office of the Status of Women, *Women in Australia*, Canberra, June 2003 p. 7.

13   Natasha Cortis and Eileen Newmarch, 'Boys in School: What's Happening?', conference paper presented to 'Manning the Next Millennium' Conference, School of Humanities and Social Sciences, Queensland University of Technology, 1–2 December 2000.

14   Matt Wade and Lisa Pryor, 'Women leading the march back into the workforce', *Sydney Morning Herald*, 11 February 2005.

15   Diana Bagnall, 'The girl power myth', *The Bulletin*, 2002, vol. 120, no. 30, p. 20.

16   Rose Herceg quoted in Clara Iaccarino, 'Girls who misbehave even better than boys', *The Sun-Herald*, 15 February 2004.

17   Michael Carr-Gregg, Kate Enderby and Sonia Grover, 'Risk-taking behaviour of young women in Australia: Screening for health-risk behaviours', *Medical Journal of Australia*, vol. 178, 16 June 2003.

18   Valerie Walkerdine quoted in Bagnall, 'The girl power myth', p. 24.

19   Hugh Mackay, *Generations: Baby boomers, their parents and their children*, Macmillan, Sydney, 1997, p. 101.

20   See Chilla Bulbeck, 'Gender Issues and the Women's Movement: Attitudes of young people in USA, Australia, Canada, China, India, Vietnam, Indonesia, Thailand, South Korea, Japan, www.arts.adelaide.edu.au/socialsciences/people/gls/gender_issues. pdf, p.2.

21   Quoted in Ellen Connolly, 'Oh sister, oh brother', *Sydney Morning Herald*, 18–19 December 2004.

22   Biddulph, *Manhood*, p. 142

23   Hugh Mackay, *The Mackay Report*, May 2003, Sydney, p. 33.

24   Peter Holmes, 'Spit and polish', *The Sunday Telegraph*, 1 June 2003.

25   Wayne Martino and Maria Pallotta-Chiarolli, *Boys' Stuff: Boys talking about what matters*, Allen & Unwin, Sydney, 2001, p. 30.

25   Letter to the editor, N. Medcalf, 'The great generation', *The Australian*, 11 January 2005.

27   Mackay, *Generations*, p. 108.

28   Lumby, *Bad Girls*, p. 78.

Chapter 4

1   Joe Lockard, 2001, 'Britney Spears, Victorian Chastity and Brand-name Virginity', *Bad Subjects* http://eserver.org/bs/57/lockardB.html [23 February 2005].

2   ibid.

3   ibid.

4   Neil Howe and William Strauss, *Millennials Rising: The Next Great Generation*, Vintage, New York, 2000, p. 197.

5   ibid., p. 190.

6   ibid., p. 189.

7   *Australian Study of Health and Relationships* is conducted by the Australian Centre in Sex, Health and Society at La Trobe

University. It is published in the *Australian and New Zealand Journal of Public Health*, vol. 27, no. 2, April 2003.

8   Doreen Rosenthal, 'Papa, don't preach, it won't be effective', *Sydney Morning Herald*, 23 June 2004.

9   ibid.

10   The *Secondary School Students and Sexual Health Report 2002* found that the majority of respondents reported 'overwhelmingly positive' feelings in relation to their most recent sexual encounter. However, just over a quarter of all sexually active students reported having had unwanted sex, due to being drunk or pressure from a partner.

11   Amanda Fairweather, 'All my friends are still getting married', *Sydney Morning Herald*, 31 December 2004.

12   Richard de Visser, Anthony Smith, Chris Rissel, Juliet Richters, Andrew Grulich, 'Safer sex and condom use among a representative sample of adults', *Australian and New Zealand Journal of Public Heath*, vol. 27, no. 2, 2003, p. 228.

13   Rick Hicks and Kathy Hicks, *Boomers, Xers and Other Strangers: Understanding the Generational Differences That Divide Us*, Tyndale, Illinois, 1999, p. 183.

14   Cosima Marriner, 'Generation Y Not', *Sydney Morning Herald*, 28 November 2003.

15   The *Secondary Students and Sexual Health Report 2002* found that young people are 'appropriately dubious' about the quality of Internet-based information regarding all topics, including sexuality or sexual health.

16   Greg Thom, 'Techno technique: Chat-up lines for our modern age', *The Daily Telegraph*, 12 February 2004.

17   See generally Chris Rissel, Juliet Richters, Andrew Grulick, Richard de Visser, Anthony Smith, 'Attitudes towards sex in a representative sample of adults', *Australian and New Zealand Journal of Public Heath*, vol. 27, no. 2, 2003.

18   ibid.; p. 120.

19   In March 2004, *Queer Eye* was one of Channel 10's most popular shows with a national average audience of 1 516 000 viewers. This included more than half of the 16–39-year-old demographic, that is Generation Y and X, straight and gay and in-between. Scott Ellis, 'Gay and here to stay', *The Sun-Herald*, 21–27 March 2004.

20   One in five gay, lesbian or bisexual people have children. Susan Pitman with Tania Herbert, Clare Land and Cas O'Neil, *Profile of Young Australians: Facts, Figures & Issues*, Foundation for Young Australians, Melbourne, 2003, p. 6.

21   The Democrats Youth Poll 2003 found 78 per cent of young people supported equal rights for gay men and lesbians. This figure has remained relatively stable according to the Poll: 77 per cent in 2001 and 80 per cent in 2002.

22   Special Poll: Australians Say Homosexuality Not Immoral But Americans Evenly Divided. See www.roymorgan.com finding no. 3429, 7 August 2001.

23   Bulbeck, 'Gender Issues and the Women's Movement', p. 4. (The *Sex in Australia* and *Secondary School and Sexual Health 2002* reports came to the same conclusion.)

24   Catharine Lumby, *Bad Girls: The media, sex and feminism in the 90s*, Allen & Unwin, Sydney, 1997, p. 85.

25   Rissel et al., 'Attitudes towards sex', p. 188.

26   ibid., p. 122.

Chapter 5

1   Dominic Knight argues that for people in their mid-20s, the hard edge of Generation Y, 'early' marriage is taking off as it provides a stable emotional life for young people who are living risky and demanding professional lives. Dominic Knight, 'The mild ones', The *Sun Herald*, 17 October 2004.

2   Information provided to author by editor of *Cosmo Bride*, Frankie Hobson, via email.

3   Susan Pitman with Tania Herbert, Clare Land and Cas O'Neil, *Profile of Young Australians: Facts, Figures & Issues*, Foundation for Young Australians, Melbourne, 2003, p. 7.

4   See <www.abs.gov.au>.

5   Bernard Salt, 'The X, Y factor', *Business Review Weekly*, 16–22 September 2004.

6   Amanda Fairweather, 'All my friends are still getting married', *Sydney Morning Herald*, 23 June 2004.

7 See www.abs.gov.au.

8 Pitman et al., *Profile of Young Australians*, p. 21.

9 Claire Cartwright, 'Life Stories of Young Adults Who Experienced Parental Divorce as Children and Adolescents', conference paper presented at the 9th Australian Institute of Family Studies Conference, Melbourne, Australia, 2005, p. 3.

10 Indeed, Cartwright argues that one of the more positive effects of parental separation is that children feel life is better after the divorce and they themselves felt 'stronger, more mature, independent and tolerant of others as a result'. Cartwright, 'Life Stories of Young Adults, p. 4. Divorce has given these Yers closure that Yers from intact but unhappy families haven't experienced.

11 Vox pop, 'Why are people getting married later these days?', *The Sun-Herald*, 29 February 2004.

12 Adele Horin, 'Romance and the me generation', *Sydney Morning Herald*, 10 April 2004.

13 Pitman et al., *Profile of Young Australians*, p. 7.

14 See www.abs.gov.au.

15 Pitman et al., *Profile of Young Australians*, p. 18.

16 Horin, 'Romance and the me generation'.

17 Rachel Hills, 'It's possible to do everything, but it's easier to do nothing', *Sydney Morning Herald*, 3 February 2005.

18 Neil Howe and William Strauss, *Millennials Rising: The Next Great Generation*, Vintage, New York, 2000, p. 130.

19 Quoted in Adele Horin, 'Cautious and picky young singles put marriage on the backburner', *Sydney Morning Herald*, 22 September 2004.

Chapter 6

1 High school retention rates to Year 12 have doubled since the early 1980s, and over the last decade the number of students going onto tertiary study has increased by 80 per cent. See the ABS's Youth Australia Report <www.abs.gov.au>.

2 See Neil Howe & William Strauss, *Millennials Rising: The Next Great Generation*, Vintage, New York, 2000, pp. 143–66. Y students

in Australia are being subject to similar pressures to excel. See Jane Caro, 'High expectations, high anxiety and high schools', *NewMatilda.com*, 23 February 2005, www.newmatilda.com.au.

3 Howe & Strauss, *Millennials Rising*, p. 211.

4 Coupland defines a 'McJob' as 'a low-pay, low-prestige, low-dignity, low-benefit, no-future job in the service sector [that is] frequently considered a satisfying career choice by people who have never held one'. Douglas Coupland, *Generation X: Tales for An Accelerated Culture*, St Martin's Press, New York, 1991, p. 5.

5 Australian Bureau of Statistics Labour Force Figures for February 2005, see www.abs.gov.au. More broadly, half the world's unemployed are under 24, according to the International Labor Organisation. Although young people represent 25 per cent of the working age population, they make up as much as 47 per cent of the 186 million people out of work worldwide in 2003. 'Youth Unemployment at All-Time High', *Brainbox*, 15 April 2005, www.brainbox.com.au.

6 Phillip Toner argues that had this sustained decline in the training rate over the last decade not occurred, there would be nearly 19 000 job opportunities available for young people aged 15–24. Phillip Toner, 'Declining Apprentice Training Rates: Causes, Consequences and Solutions', Research paper, Industry Studies, University of Western Sydney, July 2003.

7 Jared Bernstein, 'The Young and the Jobless', *The American Prospect*, October 2003, p. 17.

8 David Brooks, 'The Organization Kid', *The Atlantic Monthly*, April 2002, www.theatlantic.com.

9 Pitman et al. found that 'the amount of time students overall are working is increasing with potential detrimental effects on their study'. Susan Pitman et al., *Profile of Young Australians: Facts, Figures & Issues*, Foundation for Young Australians, Melbourne, 2003, p. 4

10 Ebru Yaman, 'On pay, students mean business', *The Australian*, 17 November 2004. Many university students now pay $20 000 for a science degree, $40 000 for a law degree and nearly $15 000 for an arts degree.

11 Pitman et al., *Profile of Young Australians*, p. 4.

12 On the rising cost of buying and renting property in Australia, see

generally Marion Powell and Glenn Withers, 'National Summit on Housing Affordability' resource paper, Canberra, 27–29 June 2004, www.appliedeconomics.com.au. In 2003 housing affordability across Australia slipped to its lowest level in 13 years. First-home buyers must now put aside 25.3 per cent of their income to meet mortgage repayments. CPM Research argues that 'the recent rise in housing prices can be attributed to the decreased number of first-home buyers in the market'. The fact that young Australians face serious difficulty buying a home has affected the entire market, driving up prices for everyone. CPM Research, 'Housing affordability falls to 13 year low', 20 July 2003, www.propertyweb.com.au.

13 Pitman et al., *Profile of Young Australians*, p. 25.

14 Coupland, *Generation X*, p. 143.

15 In 2001, 62 per cent of young people aged 15 to 24 lived at home. Pitman et al., *Profile of Young Australians*, p. 7.

16 See <www.democrats.org.au>.

17 Pitman et al., *Profile of Young Australians*, p. 5.

18 Coupland's term for the 'feelings of jealousy in the young and the disenfranchised when facing gruesome housing statistics'. Coupland, *Generation X*, p. 144. Its cousin is 'Boomer envy', that 'envy of material wealth and long-range material security accrued by older members of the baby boom generation by virtue of fortunate births'. ibid., p. 21.

19 Pitman et al., *Profile of Young Australians*.

20 Adele Horin and Alexa Moses, 'The class of '91 grows up', *Sydney Morning Herald*, 18 June 2003.

21 Naomi Klein argues that 'there is no question that many young people have compensated for the fact that they don't trust politicians or corporations by adopting the social-Darwinist values of the system that engendered their insecurity.' Naomi Klein, *No Logo*, pp. 267–8. In other words, Yers believe the system won't look after them but rather than demand more from government and corporations, they expect less and instead take an individualist view on how to survive this uncaring and hostile world.

22 Catherine Allen, 'Y You Should Care!', *Employment Review*, December 2002/January 2003.

23 Fullilove and Flutter describe these Yers as 'rite of passage

travellers'. 'These young Australians tend to be away for shorter periods, often on working holiday visas, and split their time between work and travel.' Michael Fullilove and Chloë Flutter, *Diaspora: The World Wide Web of Australians*, Lowy Institute Paper 04, Longueville, Sydney, 2004, p. 21. Fullilove and Flutter explored the growing Australian dysphoria of young, often well-educated, workers who either move overseas permanently or spend a good slice of their early to mid-careers working overseas.

24 The attitudes and behaviours of Yers to the world of work present a particular challenge to trade unions. Because Yers move in and out of professions and workplaces and are employed in hard-to-unionise sectors, they are difficult for unions to reach and retain. Their acceptance of job insecurity and dog-eat-dog attitude to career success doesn't help. The statistics are evidence of this. Only 18 per cent of young people joined a union in 2002. Pitman et al., *Profile of Young Australians*, p. 35.

25 See <www.pophouse.com.au>.

26 Brigid Delaney, 'The Young and the Restless', *Sydney Morning Herald*, 23 October 2004.

27 Bonnie Malkin, 'Generation flex', *Sydney Morning Herald*, 26 July 2003.

28 Alan Mascaredbhas, 'The 70-Hour Week', *Sydney Morning Herald*, 8 December 2004.

29 Mark McCrindle, 'Understanding Generation Y', *Prime Focus*, May 2003.

30 Annabel Stafford, 'A generation so good at saying no', *Australian Financial Review*, 22 March 2005. That being said, a survey of 7500 people by recruitment firm Hudson found that it was Xers who nominated 'more interesting work' as the single biggest motivating factor in terms of employment, whereas Generation Y were 'more materialistic' and were inspired to work for 'better money'. Jackie Woods, *Sydney Morning Herald*, 28 July 2004. My view is that if given a choice, some Yers might opt for more money for boring work and find fun and stimulation outside the office.

31 Barbara Pocock, 'Work and Family Futures: How Young Australians plan to work and care', Australia Institute discussion paper no. 69, August 2004, p. vi. See www.barbarapocock.com.au.

32 ibid., p. vi.

33 Shapiro Barash quoted in Caroline Overington, 'When marriage *is* the career', *Sydney Morning Herald*, 24–25 January 2004.

34 Bittman and Thompson's work on men's uptake of family-friendly employment provisions amongst older male workers shows that 'while an increasing number of men know they should and want take on more domestic responsibilities, there is a gap between what men say they want and what they actually do (or fail to do)'. Their research shows that take-up rates for Australian men of these provisions are low. 'In 1999, only 18 per cent of fathers used flexible hours to balance work and family and 73 per cent did not use a single family-friendly provision. A mere 2 per cent of men indicated that they had switched to part-time work for child care reasons.' M. Bittman and D. Thompson, *Men's uptake of family-friendly employment provisions*, Policy Research Paper no. 22, Department of Family and Community Services, Canberra, 2004, p. 1, ix.

35 Pocock argues that if this door doesn't fall open, young men will 'leave the nurturing to their partners, the default carers'. Pocock, 'Work and Family Futures', p. vi.

Chapter 7

1 Douglas Coupland, *Generation X: Tales for an Accelerated Culture*, St Martins Press, New York, 1991, p. 80.

2 Hunter S. Thompson, *Fear and Loathing on the Campaign Trail '72*, Flamingo, London, 1994, p. 61.

3 Ariadne Vromen, "People Try to Put Us Down": Participatory Citizenship of "Generation X", *Australian Journal of Political Science*, vol. 38, no. 1, 2003, p. 81

4 Neil Howe and William Strauss, *Millennials Rising: The Next Great Generation*, Vintage, New York, 2000, p. 46–7.

5 Joyce Chia and Glenn Patmore, 'The Vocal Citizen', Glenn Patmore (ed), *The Vocal Citizen*, Arena, Melbourne, 2004, p. 3.

6 Murray Print, Larry Saha and Kathy Edwards, 'Youth Electoral Study: Enrolment and Voting', research paper, December 2004, p. 2. See www.aec.gov.au. Furthermore 'in countries where voting

is not compulsory, youth enrolment and voting is invariably the lowest of any age group'. Print et al., 'Enrolment and Voting', pp. 3–4.

7   Mark Coultan, 'Big bother', *Sydney Morning Herald*, 19–20 June 2004. Coultan argues that the young audience's aggressive response to a political protest about refugees by a contestant on the reality TV show *Big Brother* is evidence of that generation's antagonism to politics in general. Whilst I would question Coultan's conclusions, he does make the good point that conventional protests aren't very popular with young people. They respond better to more creative and humorous expressions of political dissent as exercised by people like Mike Moore and the filmmaker Morgan Spurlock.

8   All political parties guard details about their membership with some fierceness. This information was found out through personal contacts on the proviso I didn't acknowledge sources.

9   W. J. Stone, R. B. Rapoport and Monique B. Schneider, 'Party Members in a Three-Party Election', *Party Politics*, vol. 10, no. 4, 2004, p. 450.

10   W. Cross and L. Young, 'The Contours of Political Party Membership in Canada', *Party Politics*, vol. 10, no. 4, 2004, p. 432.

11   Simon Castles, 'No one is talking to young voters', *Sydney Morning Herald*, 14 April 2004.

12   ibid.

13   Print et al. came to similar conclusions. 'Youth are typically stereotyped as politically apathetic. That is not what we found. They were interested in political issues, what to them were *real* issues, though, not political parties and politicians.' Print et al., 'Enrolment and Voting', p. 23.

14   George Barna, *Generations Next: What You Need to Know About Today's Youth*, Regal, Ventura, 1995, p. 46.

15   Catharine Lumby, *Gotcha: Life in a Tabloid World*, Allen & Unwin, Sydney, 1999, p. 146.

16   Amongst the traditional news media, TV news was rated the best and most popular amongst young adults. Jason Sternberg, 'Rating youth: A statistical review of young Australians' news media use', *Australian Studies in Journalism*, vol. 7, 1998, pp. 84, 101.

17   ibid., p. 122.

18   Howe and Strauss, *Millennials Rising*, p. 232. This is one of
      Catharine Lumby's main arguments in her book *Gotcha*, that
      populist even trashy media forums like women's magazines and
      talk shows are important sites for political discussion and
      contestation. Print et al. came to some slightly different
      conclusion, finding that TV and newspapers were significant
      sources of information about voting, whereas the quality of
      information on the Internet was treated with real scepticism.
      Print et al., 'Enrolment and Voting', p. 13.

19   Over the 2000–03 period, the Democrats Youth Poll showed that
      well over 50 per cent of young people ranked family as the most
      trustworthy source of political information compared with
      politicians who consistently ranked less than 10 per cent. See
      www.democrats.org.au. Print et al. also found parents and
      teachers were important sources of political information for
      young people, with the vast majority of students considering
      politicians to be untrustworthy. Print et al., 'Enrolment and
      Voting', pp. 13, 21.

20   Clive Hamilton, *Growth Fetish*, Allen & Unwin, Sydney, 2003, p. 21.

21   Lumby, *Gotcha*, p. xix.

22   ibid., p. 154.

23   Vromen, 'People Try to Put Us Down', p. 82. Vromen's findings are
      backed up by successive Democrats Youth Polls which show that
      over the 2000–03 period, 60–68 per cent of young Australians
      were involved in volunteer work such as environmental work,
      fundraising, teaching/instructing, coaching, counselling, food
      preparation, youth development, sport-recreation and emergency
      services. Statistics from Volunteering Australia show that on
      average young people volunteered 60.5 hours of their time per
      year, mainly for reasons of personal satisfaction and to help
      others in the community rather than to gain new skills or work
      experience. See www.volunteeringaustralia.org.

24   Drake Bennett, 'Doing Disservice', *The American Prospect*, October
      2003, p. 20.

25   Susan Pitman, Tania Herbert, Claire Land and Cas O'Neil, *Profile
      of Young Australians: Facts, Figures and Issues*, Foundation for
      Young Australians, Melbourne, 2003, p. 11. See
      www.youngaustralians.org/profile.

26 Naomi Klein, *No Logo*, Flamingo, London, 2001, p. xix.

27 As of March 2004, available data shows that 11 per cent of total financial members of Amnesty International Australia were aged 18–25 years. In addition 21 per cent of all Human Rights Defenders, who pledge monthly donations, were in that age bracket. Similarly in the period between January and March 2004, 47 per cent of all volunteers working with Oxfam Australia were aged between 17 and 25. Thanks to Dianna Andoni from Amnesty International (Australia) and Lucy Quarterman from Oxfam Community Aid Abroad (Australia) for these figures.

28 The Australian Greens suggest its voter cohort consists of 36.9 per cent youth (voters aged 18–24 years). Pitman et al., *Profile of Young Australians*, p.18.

29 Anna Greenberg, 'New Generation, New Politics', *The American Prospect*, October 2003, p. 4.

30 Howe and Strauss, *Millennials Rising*, p. 185.

31 T. Watts, H. Martin and F. Stewart, 'Debunking the Great Generation X Myth', *The Age*, 29 January 2002.

32 Greenberg, 'New Generation, New Politics', p. 3.

33 ibid., p. 4. It is not surprising that young people aren't supportive of a welfare system that many of them believe will be gone once they reach old age. A 1995 Luntz survey conducted in the United States found that 46 per cent of Generation X believed in UFOs but only 37 per cent of them believed social security would exist by the time they retired. Generation Y are the same—they know that whilst their taxes might fund the Boomers' retirement, they won't be so lucky.

34 ibid, p. 4.

Chapter 8

1 Rosalind Wiseman, *Queen Bees and Wannabes: Helping your daughter survive cliques, gossip, boyfriends and other realities of adolescence*, Random House, London, 2003, p. 77.

2 See Eating Disorder Association Resource Centre <www.uq.net.au/eda>.

3 See Australian Longitudinal Women's Health Study www.newcastle.edu.au/centre/wha/study.

4 See Eating Disorder Association Resource Centre <www.uq.net.au/eda>.

5 See <www.womhealth.org.au>.

6 Rachael Oakes Ash, *Anything She Can Do I Can Do Better*, Random House, Sydney, 2004.

7 See generally Catharine Lumby, *Bad Girls: Media, sex and feminism in the 90s*, Allen & Unwin, Sydney, 1997, p. 3.

8 Alissa Quart, *Branded: The Buying and selling of teenagers*, Arrow, London, 2003, p. 150.

9 Wiseman, *Queen Bees & Wannabes*, pp. 80–1.

10 Pru Goward, *Body Images and Eating Awareness: A Guide to Developing Groups for Adult Women*, Victorian Health Promotion Foundation, Victoria, 1992, p. 13.

11 Peter West, *What's the matter with boys?: Showing boys the way towards manhood*, Choice, Sydney, 2002, p. 152.

12 Quart makes the point that 'becoming a branded boy body takes just as much labour and pain as becoming a branded girl body.' Quart, *Branded*, pp. 172–3.

13 Peter West, 'From Tarzan to the Terminator: Boys, Men and Body Image', conference paper presented at The Institute of Family Studies Conference, Sydney, 24 July 2000, pp. 5, 13.

14 Murray Drummond, 'Bodies: A REAL Emerging Issue for Boys and Young Men', *Everybody*, vol. 2, August 1998.

15 See <www.internationalnodietday.com>.

16 *A Current Affair*, Channel 9, 'Eating disorders: The male maelstrom', 6 December 2002, <www.aca.ninemsn.com>. The Eating Disorder Association Resource Centre puts the figure slightly lower at 5 per cent. See <www.uq.net.au/eda>.

17 Quart, *Branded*, p. 173.

18 West, 'From Tarzan to the Terminator', p. 13. See also Quart, *Branded*, p. 172.

19 *Dimensions*, Australian Broadcasting Commission, 'Male Body Image', Episode 14 (transcript) 1 October 2002.

20 This pressure exerted on young men by women even extends to cosmetic surgery. Dr Colin Moore, a Sydney penis-enlargement specialist, says many of his young clients come forward on their

partner's insistence. He says 'Today's young women are more forthright . . . they know what they want and they demand it.' Patrick Carlyon, 'The price of perfection', *The Bulletin*, 2 June 2004.

21 Naomi Wolf, *The Beauty Myth: How Images of Beauty are Used Against Women*, Vintage, London, 1990, p. 252.

22 ibid., p. 218.

23 Brigid Delaney, 'The shape of things to come', *Sydney Morning Herald*, 8–9 January 2005.

24 ibid. Also, Quart reports that in only one year, from 2000 to 2001, the number of cosmetic surgeries on teens 18 and under increased 21.8 per cent. Quart, *Branded*, p. 146.

25 *A Current Affair*, 'Cosmetic surgery: Does age really matter?', <www.ninemsn.com.au>, 30 May 2003. This mirrors a growing trend in cosmetic surgery in all age groups. The Australian Society of Plastic Surgeons estimates that in 2003, 70 000 Australians underwent cosmetic plastic surgery, a 32 per cent increase from 2002. Suzanne Walker, 'Saving Face', *Vogue Australia*, September 2004.

26 Walker, 'Saving Face'.

27 Quart, *Branded*, p. 155.

28 ibid., p. 155.

29 ibid., p. 149.

30 Alf Lewis quoted in Delaney, 'The shape of things to come'. Similarly, even those Y girls who don't want anything done to their current body wouldn't rule it out after pregnancy. Like Kerry, who would consider cosmetic surgery if her body became 'disfigured' after having children. In fact, Gen Y girls who have had children are the most vocal about how unhappy they are with their bodies and how much they would like to surgically alter them. They talk about how they can't wear the midriff-bearing tops that their friends can.

31 Quart, *Branded*, p. 151.

32 Celebrity flesh flashing 'is at an all-time high' with female celebs currently displaying, on average, 59 per cent of their bodies when they step onto the red carpet. The figure is up from 39 per cent in 1994. 'Spike', *Sydney Morning Herald*, 6 January 2005.

33 Quart, *Branded*, pp. 161–2.

34   ibid., p. 162.
35   ibid., p. 151.
36   Catharine Lumby, *Gotcha: Life in a Tabloid World*, Allen & Unwin, Sydney, 1999, p. 18.
37   Wolf, *The Beauty Myth*, p. 247
38   ibid., p. 258.
39   See <www.monash-hospital.com.au>.
40   *Dimensions*, ABC, Male Body Image.
41   See <www.monash-hospital.com.au>.
42   Carlyon, 'The price of perfection'.
43   Quart, *Branded*, p. 115.
44   Wolf, *The Beauty Myth*, p. 252.
45   Personal email to the author.
46   Diana Bagnall, 'The girl power myth', *The Bulletin*, 2002, vol. 120, no. 30.
47   Quart, *Branded*, p. 173.
48   Lumby, *Gotcha*, p. 125.

Chapter 9

1   Later, the Internet became another important media vehicle for selling to children. In the late 1990s the director of Saatchi & Saatchi Interactive stated that 'There is probably no other product or service that we can think of that is like the Internet in terms of capturing kids' interest.' Sharon Beder, 'Marketing to Children: A Community View', 'Caring for Children in the Media Age', papers from a national conference, edited by John Squires and Tracy Newlands, New College Institute for Values Research, Sydney, 1998, p. 4.
2   Barbara Pocock and Jane Clarke, 'Can't Buy Me Love? Young Australians' views on parental work, time, guilt and their own consumption', The Australia Institute, Discussion Paper no. 61, February 2004.
3   Neil Howe and William Strauss, *Millennials Rising: The Next Great Generation*, Vintage, New York, 2000, p. 269.
4   Beder, 'Marketing to Children', p. 1.
5   ibid., p. 2.

6   Jim DeRogatis, 2001, 'What's up with Generation Y?', *Salon*, <www.salon.com> [23 March 2004].

7   Howe and Strauss, *Millennials Rising*, p. 265.

8   Mandy Thomas, 'Hanging out in Westfield Parramatta' in *Ingenious: Emerging Youth Cultures in Urban Australia*, Melissa Butcher and Mandy Thomas (eds), Pluto, Sydney, 2003, p. 102.

9   Chris Richardson, 'The generation gap', *Business Review Weekly*, 16–22 September 2004.

10 Some 93 per cent of 21-year-old Americans have a credit card, up from 60 per cent just five years ago. The average 21-year-old is carrying almost $3000 in credit card debt, with 10 per cent with balances exceeding $7000. Michael J Weiss, 'To Be About To Be' *American Demographics*, 1 September 2003. A survey by the NSW Office of Fair Trading found that rising mobile phone and credit card bills have resulted in Australians aged between 18 and 24 carrying an average debt of almost $6000 (excluding HECS debt). Kirsty Needham, 'Cut credit cards call', *Sydney Morning Herald*, 25 November 2003.

11 Richardson, 'The generation gap'.

12 Douglas Coupland, *Generation X, Tales for an Accelerated Culture*, St Martin's Press, New York, 1991, p. 106.

13 Kate Crawford, 'A generations scolded for not taking options that aren't there', *Sydney Morning Herald*, 27 May 2004.

14 Alissa Quart, *Branded: the buying and selling of teenagers*, Arrow, London, 2003, p. xxiv.

15 Rick Hicks and Kathy Hicks, *Boomers, Xers and Other Strangers: Understanding the Generational Differences that Divide Us*, Tyndale, Illinois, 1999, p. 271.

16 Quart, *Branded*, p. 117.

17 ibid., p. 46.

18 Naomi Klein, *No Logo*, Flamingo, London, 2001, p. 57.

19 Susan Hopkins, *Girl Heroes: the new force in popular culture*, Pluto Press, Sydney, 2002, p. 4.

20 Clive Hamilton, *Growth Fetish*, Allen & Unwin, Sydney, 2003, p. 82.

21 Catharine Lumby, *Bad Girls: Media, sex and feminism in the 90s*, Allen & Unwin, Sydney, 1997, p. 79.

22 Hamilton, *Growth Fetish*, p. 96.

23   Quoted in Julian Lee, 'Adultescents just want to sate the wonderlust', *Sydney Morning Herald*, 25 March 2004.

24   Michael J. Weiss, 'To Be, About To Be'.

25   Hugh Mackay, *The Mackay Report: Leaving School*, Report no. 98, March 2000, p. 28.

26   ibid. p. 8.

27   The tendency for 'cool' to always shift and change has helped foster the anti-cool forms of cool such as 'geek chic'. See Judith Ireland, 'Geek Chic', *Sydney Morning Herald*, 9 February 2005.

28   Vince Mitchell, <www.umist.ac.uk>.

29   Chris Watt, 'Cool's not cool when marketing to youth', www.bandt.com.au, 11 July 2002.

30   Pocock and Clarke, 'Can't Buy Me Love', p. xi.

31   And the second greatest influence must be the family, given the nostalgic loyalty to childhood brands.

32   On peer-to-peer marketing see Quart, *Branded*, pp. 48–59. Peer-to-peer (or viral, buzz or word-of-mouth marketing, whatever variation or term used) is a marketing technique that creates or facilitates personal communication as a vehicle for product endorsement. Peer-to-peer employs influential agents to recommend products to friends, colleagues and acquaintances as a form of authentic advertising and promotion.

33   Watt, 'Cool's not cool'.

34   See <www.cass.city.ac.uk>.

35   Pocock and Clarke, 'Can't Buy Me Love', p. xi.

36   Vromen, 'People try to put us down', p. 86. Youth boycotts of sportswear companies that use third-world sweat shops are a prime example of this. See generally Klein, *No Logo*.

37   Quart, *Branded*, p. 288.

38   See <www.adbusters.com>.

Chapter 10

1   Sarah Price and Matthew Benns, 'Hillsong's True Believers', *Sun Herald*, 7 November 2004.

2   See www.hillsong.com.

3   Brigid Delaney, 'With Song in Their Hearts', *Sydney Morning Herald*, 21 January 2005.

4   Susan Pitman with Tania Herbert, Clare Land and Cas O'Neil, *Profile of Young Australians: Facts, Figures & Issues*, Foundation for Young Australians, Melbourne, 2003, p. 48.

5   From website: www.hillsong.com. See also www.hillsong.com/youth.

6   Hugh Mackay, 'Watching the sparrow', *Griffith Review*, Autumn 2005, pp. 73–8, p. 73.

7   ibid.

8   For those Yers who are steadfast church-goers, religion is a dominant force, shaping everything from their friendship circle to their voting preferences. Tim explains that being a Christian plays 'a central role' in his life, informing his 'career choices, life goals and actions'. Amongst young Jewish Australians, Jewishness is very important, although it often relates more to a certain ethnical and cultural identity rather than a theological one. Madelaine considers herself 'culturally Jewish', something that 'comes before the actual religion itself'.

9   Delaney, 'With Song in Their Hearts'.

10   Pitman et al., *Profile of Young Australians*, p. 48.

11   Data provided by Marc L'Huillier from Sweeney Research. In the Spin/Sweeney Report on 16–28-year-olds, religion was at the bottom of the 'Priorities in Life' index, even below having children, marriage and fulfilling parents' expectations. See also Carol Nader, 'Glitterazzi and burbanite alike, Generation Y makes for a complex mix', *Sydney Morning Herald*, 9 October 2003.

12   Hugh Mackay, *Generations: Baby boomers, their parents and their children*, Macmillan, Sydney, 1997, p. 114.

13   Simon Castles, 'Why I Won't Be in Church on Sunday', *The Age*, 20 March 2000.

14   Mackay, *Leaving School*, p. 25.

15   'The proportion of 15–24-year-old adherents to Buddhism, Islam and Hinduism is higher than for Christianity or Judaism with the largest group being Buddhists.' Pitman et al., *Profile of Young Australians*, p. 48.

16   Ruth Webber, 'Young people and their quest for meaning', *Youth Studies Australia*, vol. 21, no. 1, 2002, 40–43, p. 41.

17   Richard Eckersley, *Well and Good: How We Feel & Why It Matters*, Text, Melbourne, 2004, p. 3

18   Mackay, *Generations*, p. 145.

19   Eckersley, *Well and Good*, p. 3.

20   Mackay, *Generations*, p. 194.

21   Douglas Coupland, *Generation X: Tales for An Accelerated Culture*, St Martin's Press, New York, 1991, p. 74.

22   It does seem that 'young people's beliefs, ideas and expectations have more in common with parents than with their peers'. Ani Wieranga, 'Imagined trajectories: local culture and social identity' in Rob White (ed.), *Australian Youth subcultures: on the margins and in the mainstream*, Australian Clearinghouse for Youth Studies, Hobart, 1999, pp. 189–199, p. 190.

23   David Brooks, 'The Organization Kid', *The Atlantic Monthly*, April 2002, www.theatlantic.com.

24   Mackay, *Generations*, p. 146.

25   Pocock and Clarke, *Can't Buy Me Love*, p. 11.

26   Coupland, *Generation X*, p. 139.

27   Rachel Hills, 'It's possible to do everything', *Sydney Morning Herald*, 3 February 2005.

28   Neil Howe and William Strauss, *Millennials Rising: The Next Great Generation*, Vintage, New York, 2000, p. 184.

29   Brooks, 'The Organization Kid'.

30   Howe & Strauss, *Millennials Rising*, p. 187.

31   Howe and Strauss, *Generations*, p. 317. Through the 1980s, roughly 5000 children under age 18 committed suicide each year, the largest number and proportion ever recorded for that age bracket. Howe and Strauss, *Generations*, p. 326.

32   Cosima Marriner, 'Generation Y Not', *Sydney Morning Herald*, 28 November 2003.

33   Pitman et al., *Profile of Young Australians*, chapter 6, pp. 38–47.

34   National Drug Strategy Survey 2002. Drug abuse and drug use should be distinguished here. It is clear that even early on in high school, the vast majority of Yers had access to alcohol, tobacco and marijuana. Later on and after school, other drugs were also widely available, especially ecstasy. See AusStats, Australian Social Trends 2002, 'Selected risks faced by teenagers'.

35   Secondary students and sexual health study 2002. See also W. Loxley, 'Inform teenagers about alcohol, don't lecture them', *Sydney Morning Herald*, 15 July 2004.

36   Committee on Children and Young People, 'Children and Young People and the Misuse and Abuse of Prescription Drugs and over-the-counter medications', Issues Paper No. 3, May 2002, p. 3.

37   Ritalin use has increased from 1.56 million tablets prescribed in 1984 (when Xers were teens) to 19.33 million in 2001, the end of the Y stint in high school. Margaret Rice, 'New Approach to ADHD', *Sydney Morning Herald*, 13 March 2003.

38   This is part of what Ray Moynihan and Alan Cassels call 'the medicalisation of human problems'. See *Selling Sickness: How drug companies are turning us all into patients*, Allen & Unwin, Sydney, 2005, p. 76.

39   See Democrats Youth Poll (2003, 59 per cent; 2002, 53 per cent; 2001, 51 per cent; 2000, 60 per cent). Whilst boys are still more likely to commit suicide, girls attempt suicide more often than boys and are more likely to be admitted to hospital with self-inflicted injuries. Girls are also more likely to engage in self-harm such as cutting.

Chapter 11

1   Douglas Coupland, *Generation X: Tales for an Accelerated Culture*, St Martin's Press, New York, 1997, pp. 3, 86.

2   David Brooks, 'The Organization Kid', the *Atlantic Monthly*, April 2002, <www.theatlantic.com>.

3   See <www.bca.com.au>.

4   Debra Jopson, 'Not long out of nappies—and that's the mums', *Sydney Morning Herald*, 9 February 2004.

5   Susan Pitman with Tania Herbert, Clare Land and Cas O'Neil, *Profile of Young Australia: Facts, Figures & Issues*, Foundation for Young Australians, Melbourne, 2003, p. 7.

6   Barbara Pocock, 'Work and Family Futures: How Young Australians plan to work and care', discussion paper no. 61, August 2004, The Australia Institute, Canberra, 2004.

7   Pitman, *Profile of Young Australia*, p. 7.

8   See www.quarterlifecrisis.com.

9   ibid.

10 David Brooks, 'The Organization Kid'.

11 Bob Ellis, quoted in Dominic Knight, 'The mild ones', the *Sun Herald*, 17 October 2004.

12 Coupland, *Generation X*, p. 21.

Index

»

abortion, 164
Adbusters, 157
AIDS, 2, 8, 64–5, 103
alcohol, 50, 63–4, 173–4
Aniston, Jennifer, 123
Atkins diet, 123, 142

Bail, Kathy, 43–4
The Beauty Myth, 120–1, 125, 127, 133, 138, 141
Biddulph, Steve, 47, 51, 52
Big Brother, 41–2
body image
    of X men, 128–9
    of X women, 123
    of Y men, 128–33
    of Y women, 121–3
body modification, 130, 136
'Boomer envy', 186–7, 199
Boomers, 1, 6, 8, 10, 14, 20–1, 30, 38, 50, 72, 77, 78, 82, 91, 95, 99, 105, 109, 144, 163, 186–7
branding, 126, 148–52, 153–4
Brooks, David, 92, 169, 171–2, 186, 191
Buffy the Vampire Slayer, 27, 48

Bulbeck, Chilla, 44, 46, 50–1, 70
Business Council of Australia, 180

capitalism, 14, 19
Castles, Simon, 164
celebrity culture, 136–8, 206–7
Clarke, Jane, 144, 155, 156, 169–70
Cleo, 63, 65, 70, 126, 127, 149
Clinton, Bill, 66
cohabitation, 84–5
conformism, 18–20
consumption, 89, 144–8, 160–70
contraception, 63
cosmetic surgery, 133–41, 206
Cosmopolitan, 65, 75, 126, 149
Coupland, Douglas, 1, 6, 15, 24, 94, 96, 105, 147, 168, 187, 190, 198
culture-jammers, 157

Dalai Lama, 166–7
de Tocqueville, Alexis, 1
debt, 146, 208
Democrats Youth Poll, 68, 95, 109, 111, 112

dieting, 122–3
direct democracy, 108, 118
diversity, 34–5, 97
divorce, 13, 39, 78–81, 100
Dolly, 63, 121
drugs, 49, 173–4

early sexual experiences, 62, 63–4,
    195
eating disorders, 122–3, 131
Eckersley, Richard, 168
education
    and Y women, 48–9, 89
    apprenticeships, 90, 198
    campus culture, 92
    cost of, 90, 93
    private schooling, 91
    university, 90–1
Ellis, Bob, 186
email, 36, 104, 105
environmentalism, 114

Fairweather, Amanda, 62–3, 78
family, 95–6
fatherhood, attitudes towards,
    101, 182–3
feminism, 42–3, 82–3, 138
    attitudes of Gen X towards,
        43–4
    attitudes of Gen Y towards,
        42–3, 22, 192–3
financial security, 180–1
freedom of choice, 16, 34, 39, 69,
    96, 107–8, 118, 168, 170–1
Friends, 26–7
friendship, 25–7, 151, 154–5
    and Gen X, 34–5
    between Y men, 32–4

between Y women, 30–2
future, attitudes towards, 84, 177
    and Gen X, 178–9

Gay and Lesbian Mardi Gras, 67
Gemmell, Nikki, 31–2
generation clash, 186–7, 190
Generation X, 1–2, 6, 7, 8, 22
    comparison with Generation Y,
        5, 8–10, 14–15, 18–19, 20, 23,
        60, 76, 100, 123, 128, 178–9
    definition of, 5
Generation Y
    childhood of, 11–13, 144–6,
        163
    comparison with Generation X,
        5, 8–10, 14–15, 19, 20, 23, 26,
        60, 76, 100, 116–17, 123, 128,
        173–4, 178–9
    comparison with the Boomers,
        20–1, 30, 39, 61, 69, 72, 77–8,
        85, 87, 92, 99, 109, 163
    definition of, 2, 10, 189
    size of, 11
Girlfriend, 121
'girlpower', 42, 48
globalisation, 17, 114
Greenberg, Anna, 116, 117–18
Greer, Germaine, 41–2

Halliwell, Geri, 123
Hamilton, Clive, 111, 150
HECS, 92–3
Hills, Rachel, 170
Hillsong church, 159–63
Holmes, Peter, 53
homophobia, 69–72

homosexuality, 33, 54, 66–72, 130–1, 195–6
Hopkins, Susan, 48, 149
Horin, Adele, 84
Hornby, Nick, 27
housework, 50–1
housing, 84, 92, 93–4, 147, 180, 198–9

impatience, 38–9, 147–8, 173
independence, 82–4
infertility, 183
insecurity, 15, 97
Internet, 104, 114, 115, 195, 203, 207

Jones, Meredith, 140–1

Klein, Calvin, 131, 133, 157
Klein, Naomi, 114–15, 133, 149, 199

L'Huillier, Marc, 163
Lockard, Joe, 58–9
Lumby, Catharine, 55, 110, 112, 141, 150

Mackay, Hugh, 9, 15, 25, 50, 52, 55, 162, 163, 165, 168
Madonna, 58–9, 67, 123
marriage, 74–7, 79–87, 196
    and Gen X, 6, 7, 76, 77, 78
    and the Boomers, 30, 56, 78–80, 99
masculinity, 52, 54–5, 55–6, 128–33
    and Gen X, 55
materialism, 167, 181–2

mateship, 32–3
media, 110–11, 125–8, 132, 152
    news media, 4, 110–12, 203
McCrindle, Mark, 99
McDonalds, 110
Men's Health, 128, 132
mental illness, 52
metrosexuals, 52–4, 55
Mitchell, Vince, 156
mobile phones, 16–17, 36–9
morality, 168–9
motherhood, 50, 182–3

Oakes-Ash, Rachael, 125
The OC, 70
optimism, 3–4, 14, 15–16, 178–80
oral sex, 66
Oxfam International Youth Parliament, 103–4

peer-to-peer marketing, 209
pessimism, 79–80, 179
    and Gen X, 8, 9, 178–9
Pocock, Barbara, 100, 144, 155, 156, 169–70
politics
    attitudes, 117–18, 202
    community, 113
    international, 114–15
    knowledge of, 106, 109
    non-government organisations, 115–16, 204
    party, 103–8, 116
pornography, 63
pressure, 171–2

Quart, Alissa, 19, 126, 128, 132, 137, 140, 141, 148, 149, 156
Quarterlife Crisis, 184–5
Queer Eye for the Straight Guy, 54, 67, 130, 195

Reality Bites, 6–7
Reclaim the Streets, 157
religion, 163–6
    church attendance, 163
resisters, 21–2, 61, 155–7

security, 39, 97
September 11, 1–5
Sex and the City, 26, 31, 147
sexual abuse, 164
sexual behaviour, 60–2, 65
and Gen X, 60
sexual relationships, 27–30
Shapiro, Susan Barash, 101
shopping, 145
shopping malls, 145–6
The Simpsons, 107
smoking, 50, 173
Spears, Britney, 58–9, 61, 67, 75, 86
Spin Sweeney Youth Report, 163, 210
spirituality, 165–7
Sternberg, Jason, 110
suicide, 52, 173–5, 212
    and Gen X, 173
Summers, Anne, 43
Super Size Me, 110

technology, 17–18, 35–6, 65, 105, 115
teen films, 19

terrorism, 1–5, 23
Thompson, Hunter S., 105
Timberlake, Justin, 59
trade unions, 200
travel, 3–4, 82, 97, 199–200
TV sitcoms, 26–7

uncertainty, 55, 177–8
unemployment, 52, 90, 97, 198

Vietnam war, 164, 186
virginity, 59–61
volunteerism, 3, 113, 203
Vromen, Ari, 113

Walkerdine, Valerie, 50
Watters, Ethan, 25
Webber, Ruth, 167
weddings, 74–5
West, Peter, 51, 129
Wierenga, Ani, 13
Wiseman, Rosalind, 30–1, 32, 121–2, 127
Wolf, Naomi, 53, 120–1, 128, 138, 140
work/life balance, 30, 98–102, 182, 201